THE POINT IS TO CHANGE IT

A MANIFESTO FOR A WORLD FIT FOR PEOPLE

j

junius

This edition first published 1996 by Junius Publications Ltd
BCM JPLtd
London WC1N 3XX

ISBN 0 948392 22 3

British Library Cataloguing in Publication Data
A catalogue record for this book is available from the British Library

Design
Alex Cameron

Cover photograph
Michael Kramer

Production
Peter Ray

Printed by
Spider Web

CONTENTS

PREFACE

It is politics, Jim, but not as we know it.

This book is the end result of a couple of years of discussion, during which we have tried to make sense of the most important political trends of our time. It is a discussion that has had continually to break new ground, to come to terms with a world which now bears little resemblance to the map which guided political thought and action for the previous 50 years.

The 1990s began with a series of global shocks: the end of the Cold War, the collapse of the Soviet Union, and the start of an economic slump in the capitalist world. The decade has continued in unpredictable style, transforming the political and intellectual scene.

The great ideological issues of the past century have all but disappeared as the millennium approaches. There is no longer a genuine left v right clash of principle over the market, militarism or anything else of substance. The social issues that until recently dominated the day-to-day political contest in Britain have also dropped from view. There is now a general acceptance of things which would once have split the nation.

For instance, the scourge of mass unemployment is today seen as a permanent, if unpleasant, fact of life. And part-time and temporary jobs, once condemned as capitalist tools for exploiting casual labour, are now more likely to be viewed as normal or even as a good thing for the workforce. A few years ago, many saw it as quite right that people would fight for higher living standards. Now there is widespread condemnation of the 'greed' of those who demand more.

Analysing and intervening in these discussions over two or three years, it has become clear to the people working around *Living Marxism* magazine that something profound has changed in political life. The issues which matter most in our time are clearly very different to those which counted yesterday. From the recognition that things ain't what they used to be, we have had to develop our ideas in new directions. The result is the innovative focus on the issues dealt with in this book.

Of course, sitting down to review the state of the world today, we could have produced a familiar list of left-wing slogans complaining about problems like unemployment, exploitation and poverty which continue to scar our society. But that would be to ignore the transformation which has taken place in the political climate, and ensure our book was out of touch before it ever reached the printer.

For those of us who want to change the way things are, and to get others to think the same way, the job is not just to describe the general ills of capitalism. We need to address the particular issues which determine how people think and act at any time. Unemployment and poverty are still with us; but if these issues do not move people now, if they do not determine who does or who supports what, then in political terms they cannot matter. And making ritual complaints about them will do nothing to improve the state of society.

At different times, different issues matter most. Each era has thrown up its own great questions which define which side you are on; the issues of the day which reveal whether you stand for freedom and justice for the majority or for the interests of a privileged elite. In mid-nineteenth century America, for example, the dominant issue was slavery. In Britain a century ago, it was the exploitation of the industrial working class. These were the issues which moved people in their day, the most important questions which separated those on the side of right from the rest, and inspired struggles for a better world. If we were writing this manifesto in other times, these would have been the issues on which we would have had to take our stand.

Ask what the equivalent defining issue might be today, however, and the answer is a lot less obvious. There is very little sense of a clear divide between left and right, or between parties representing different social classes. Political issues seem to be posed with far less clarity than they used to be.

There is no great clash of competing visions of the future for humanity. Instead, all shades of opinion within mainstream politics now appear to agree that there is no alternative. That general lack of belief in the possibility of changing things for the better has itself become the central issue of our times.

Every discussion now seems to be dominated by a debilitating culture of limits. Whether the debate is about the economy, science or social policy, there is an assumption that we are no longer capable of making much progress, of improving the human condition. Indeed it is often assumed that even trying to change things is likely to make matters worse, since it will only create new risks to health, safety and the environment.

The culture of limits is now accepted as gospel by those who would see themselves on the left and the right alike. There is a constant inflation of the dangers and problems which people face today, coupled with a diminished sense of humanity having the ability to develop society and to tackle any difficulties we might come up against in the process. People are now more likely to be viewed as problems than as potential problem-solvers. When we are not being patronised as hapless, fragile victims in need of protection from life, we are being warned of 'the beast within us all' that needs to be caged and repressed.

The diminished sense of the human potential for changing the world and improving the conditions of life is now the most important issue of our age; yet in a sense it is not at issue at all, since nobody is contesting it. That is all the more reason to make the culture of limits the central focus of this book.

The manifesto which follows does not contain the kind of arguments and issues some might expect from a book with 'Marxism' on its cover. We are no less fervent than ever in our rejection of capitalist exploitation, our criticism of a society which puts profit before human needs, or our opposition to the system of global imperialism that condemns millions to misery. These and more remain critical problems that have to be tackled if we are all to have the life we want.

The biggest problem of all today, however, is that none of these social problems is susceptible to a solution unless the culture of limits is questioned and a challenge to it is put at the top of the agenda. If we accept that people are essentially vulnerable little victims incapable of taking control of affairs, then we have no chance of coming up with an answer to anything from unemployment to imperialism. While the culture of limits holds, there really can be no alternative.

There is no shortage today of people willing to criticise aspects of capitalist society, such as its impact on the natural environment. But, if it begins from the assumption that there is no alternative, such criticism can only add to the mood of pessimism and despair. The contemporary critics of the status quo are falling down on two counts. They are constantly problem-mongering, inflating the dangers and difficulties which face us in every field from food and health to science and technology. Yet when the most dangerous issue of our age emerges—the culture of limits— they do not even recognise it as a problem, but embrace it. As a result, their criticisms only spread doom and gloom about the prospects for humanity, while reinforcing the sense of people being powerless to do anything much about it. With critics like that, the capitalist elite does not need many friends.

Which is why, at *Living Marxism,* we see our job today as doing much more than criticising capitalism. That is the easy bit. There is a more pressing need to criticise the fatalistic critics, to counter the doom-mongers and put a positive case for human action in pursuit of social liberation. Many of the issues and arguments which this book centres on might fall outside the parameters of what has conventionally been seen as politics. But dealing with these unconventional questions, and puncturing the anti-human prejudices which surround them, is the precondition for making political action possible in our time. And the aim of our book is to inspire its readers to act for change. It is a manifesto for a world fit for people.

The book draws on the arguments that have been tested and refined over many issues of *Living Marxism,* and should rightly be seen as the work of all who have contributed to the development of our analysis. It is founded on the understanding that revolutionary politics have to evolve if they are to be relevant to the changed times in which we live. Some principles drawn from the past, however, can hold good for today. To paraphrase an old German, Karl Marx: the philosophers only complain about the world in various ways, but the point is to change it.

Mick Hume
Editor, *Living Marxism*

INTRODUCTION

1

Humanity has faced problems throughout history. The only difference today is that so few of us believe we can do anything about it.

A Gallup poll published in April 1996 revealed that a majority of young people in Britain (54 per cent) want the Queen to have a bigger say in how the country is run. Almost half of 16 to 34-year olds think she would make a better prime minister than John Major, while 39 per cent said she would make a better prime minister than Labour leader Tony Blair.

The fact that so many young people would rather be governed by a 70-year old hereditary monarch than by an elected politician (including this year's model, Tony Blair) is a telling sign of the depth of disaffection with the political system today. A case of 'Democracy is dead, long live the Queen'.

On the eve of another general election, the mainstream parties and their politics have never seemed so far removed from most people's lives. While MPs in the rarefied atmosphere of Westminster await the return of the elusive 'feelgood factor', many in the real world outside are feeling thoroughly unwell about the state of society. Yet there is an overpowering sense that nothing much can be done about it, and a conviction that changing the government will change little else.

The great ideological 'isms' of modern politics—welfare socialism, popular capitalism—have long since fallen into disrepute and out of favour. They have been replaced by isms of a very different sort—cynicism, pessimism, fatalism—in an age when few can see anything much worth believing in.

Few tears need be shed for the old politics, which have held society back for a century or more. But for those who want to change things for the better, today's anti-political mood also poses new problems. It represents not just the withdrawal of support from a particular government or set of policies, but a deeper loss of faith in even the possibility of political action, and a diminishing belief that people can act together to shape the future. This fatalistic mood is the biggest obstacle to any attempt to change the way the world is run. So what is to be done about it?

To challenge this mood we need to cut through the mystifications which surround public discussion today, identify the real problems that confront us, and open up the debate about how to tackle them. This book is intended as a step in that direction.

Watching the doom-laden news broadcasts these days, you could be forgiven for thinking that those sad characters carrying 'The End of the World is Nigh' sandwich boards were the sane ones after all. As the twentieth century nears its end, the feeling grows that the history of humanity as we know it may well also be drawing to a close.

The consensus among the experts is that we are besieged by new dangers, risks and uncertainties. Everything is 'in crisis'—the environment, the economy, the political system, the monarchy, the community, the family, even humanity itself. While population growth is said to threaten the destruction of the planet, reports of declining sperm counts raise the spectre of human extinction. Everything seems to be a problem, and every problem seems to be getting worse. When did you last hear a report which claimed that a problem—whether it be child abuse, heart disease or road deaths—was decreasing? Instead, it seems that the perils of everyday life are all increasing exponentially, leaving us facing new and more menacing dangers at every turn.

Not only do we appear to be living in a horror movie, but we are cast in the role of the helpless victims who are about to enter the attic where the monster lurks. In peril from the cradle to the grave, we are now reportedly under growing threat from the sun (ozone depletion, skin cancer), the air that we breath (passive smoking, car exhaust fumes), the food that we eat (cholesterol, listeria, mad cow disease) and from many of the people that we meet (child abuse, bullying, sexual harassment, domestic violence, AIDS, elder abuse and so on).

Caution is the watchword of our insecure times. Be careful about what you eat and drink and watch on TV; worry about the air that you breath and the cigarettes that your colleague smokes; keep an eye on the neighbours who talk to your children and the ones who shout at their own; look over your shoulder at every corner, unless there is a surveillance camera to do it for you. Take out a personal pension by the time you are out of your teens and think seriously about getting more personal insurance—against ill-health, unemployment, accidents, death, against everyday life. Have only safer sex, if you must have it at all, and always follow the principle that if you don't know for sure that something is safe, then don't do it. It is as if the point of living has been reduced to simply staying alive; as if the simple act of survival itself should now be looked upon as a lifetime's achievement. Indeed it is now widely accepted that to be 'a survivor' of some kind of abuse or self-abuse is a medal to be worn with pride.

We have surely entered a grim era when the things that make life physically possible—air, food, sunlight—and which make it socially viable and enjoyable—other people—are seen primarily as a threat that we need to be guarded against. The cautious, uncertain mood of the times was well captured by the 1995 advertising campaign for a major health charity which depicted the human heart, traditionally regarded as the source of vitality and the symbol of love, as 'Britain's biggest killer'. If we are now supposed to live in fear of our own internal organs, it is little wonder that the *X-Files* series about paranormal experiences (slogan: 'Trust no-one') should become the hottest thing on television.

The preoccupation with risk and the commitment to caution inevitably encourage a conservative outlook in society. In every field from science to economics, too many people are wary of change, fearful of experimenting, unwilling to adopt the old attitude of 'suck it and see'. Of course, this does not mean that nothing changes. Far from it: dramatic changes are taking place in many areas. But there is also an overpowering feeling among many people that change is out of their, or indeed anybody's, control.

Many intellectuals and media commentators are impressed by the impact of trends such as the 'globalisation' of economic affairs, or the creation of a global communications superhighway. Yet they often appear to regard these trends almost as natural processes, like the changing weather. There is no sense that a government or any other human agency could effectively direct or control them. Change has ceased to be seen in an active, positive light, as something that people can make happen. It is regarded instead with passivity and trepidation, as something that happens to people whether they like it or not.

Today's climate of caution and uncertainty provides fertile ground for the growth of a nostalgic attitude towards the past and a desire to restore what has been lost. The sense of loss is almost palpable, reinforcing the conviction that everything is getting worse. What does the future hold for a society in which some want to live in the past and many seem scared of life in the present? There is no vision of a brave new world on offer. Instead we are faced with a world of ever-lowering horizons, and hedged in with advice about what we can or should *not* do.

Anybody who thinks that it is possible to change the world and improve the human condition, who believes that tomorrow does not have to be like today, is forced to stand against the stream of contemporary society. This makes it all the more important that we set about challenging the prevailing morbid outlook, and setting out an alternative way of looking at problems and potential solutions.

To listen to today's discussions of the woes of the world, you would think that humanity had never faced any problems before. It is almost as if those running things or analysing issues today were the first generation to experience any difficulties or to have to adapt to change.

'How can we teach people the necessary parenting skills?', they ask, or 'What should people be told to eat?'. A question which is really worth asking, however, is this: how did humans ever survive through the centuries without the assistance of today's armies of counsellors, advisory committees and experts to tell them the correct way to bring up their children or feed themselves?

7

The capacity of individuals and society in general to adapt to difficult circumstances, to overcome adversity and just get on with life, seems continually to be underestimated in the panic to problematise everything today. Yet the record shows that humanity has consistently demonstrated the ingenuity and adaptability not just to survive, but to move on to bigger and better things. What has changed today is not so much the scale of the problems, but the pessimism with which society perceives its difficulties, real and imagined.

Down the centuries, people around the world have faced considerable barriers, often far worse than those problems which are viewed with such an air of doom and gloom today. In times past, for example, hunger was not the rare and scandalous problem it is today, but the normal state of affairs for most. The 'problem' of over-eating and obesity, which we are now told afflicts large portions of the population in Britain or America, is one which our predecessors would have given much to suffer. It is a problem which has been made possible by the enormous advances in agricultural methods over the past 200 years.

Disease, too, was a far more deadly threat in the past to societies which did not have the living standards to reduce vulnerability and slow its spread nor the medical capacity to prevent or cure it. The plagues of the Middle Ages, which wiped out up to a third of the population of Europe, have no equivalent in the modern world. Recent scares about 'new plagues' sweeping the planet are a mixture of the entirely unfounded and the wildly exaggerated.

What should really be shouted from the rooftops is the remarkable successes of medical science in eradicating old diseases like smallpox and in drastically reducing the scale of other epidemic diseases like cholera and typhoid. What should really be a cause of deep concern is not the hypothetical prospect of 'uncontrollable' new plagues, but the fact that relatively easily preventable and treatable conditions like tuberculosis, gastro-enteritis and malaria continue to kill millions every year, simply because of poverty and the lack of clean water and basic medical treatment.

Humanity has always been faced with problems of hunger, want, disease and death. The progress made against these foes has certainly not been in a line curving constantly upwards on the graph of history. What has been constant, however, is the way in which societies have struggled to overcome their difficulties using ingenuity, experience and technology. The advance of human enterprise and endeavour turned the sea from a mysterious barrier into a means of transport and a rich source of food and mineral wealth. It turned nature from a mystical threat into a manageable resource, in the process creating the potential capacity to feed the world many times over. Through the struggle to overcome problems, countless new possibilities for progress have been spotted and, often, realised.

What is different today is not the number of problems we face, nor the scale of the dangers confronting us. It is the fatalistic spirit with which they are approached. There is a widespread acceptance that we cannot overcome 'the environmental crisis' or 'the crisis of community' through the traditional means of economic and social development. Instead, we are told that we need to retrench, cut back, and take cover. The loudest demand of our times is that we must accept that there are now new limits to what can be achieved.

The notion that it is no longer possible to solve the problems facing people and the planet is really based not on an identification of new and insuperable difficulties, but on a novel underestimation of human capabilities. After all, why should we accept that society can no longer rise to the occasion as it has done on countless occasions before? Why should we be less able to adapt to the predicted global warming than our forefathers were able to cope with highly dramatic climatic changes?

Are we really supposed to believe that people today are more stupid or less potentially creative than their predecessors? That makes little sense. Indeed, would it not make more sense to suggest that, with the benefit of the experience and knowledge gathered by past generations, the thinkers and doers of today ought to be able to achieve what nobody has been able to do before? The problem here is not a loss of ability, but a loss of faith in the capacity of humanity to adapt, change and move on.

One of the ironies of our current predicament is that, despite the prevailing gloom, in terms of technical and scientific achievements, society is still making strides forward. The world does not stand still just because some people start panicking about the environment or global warming. Yet today's advances take place amid a mood of pessimism. At the same time as dramatic breakthroughs are being made, serious questions are being asked about whether such progress is really possible or, perhaps more importantly, whether it is even desirable.

The achievements and creations of humanity, which in other times might have been seen as a source of pride, are not widely appreciated today. Instead, anything new immediately comes under public suspicion. Indeed suspicion is not reserved for new inventions or utopian visions of the future. No, in these cautious days many have come to doubt past advances and have become reluctant to take advantage of them. The assumption is that tampering with the 'natural' order is asking for trouble, so it is best to leave everything alone.

The mood of caution is most apparent in the fields of science and technology. Here, the spirit of adventure and experimentation has been replaced by one of retrenchment and retreat. Many of the major breakthroughs of recent centuries, developments which have helped to transform human existence and lay the foundations for modern civilisation, are now being seriously called into question. Newer, less tested developments tend to be viewed with even greater suspicion and mistrust.

Inventions which have transformed people's lives for the better are now seen as a threat to our well-being. The motor car, which has helped to give millions an unprecedented degree of mobility, is now looked down upon as a public menace which kills children, pollutes the atmosphere and destroys the environment. The animal experiments which have contributed enormously to the advance of medical science are now shunned as immoral. The contraceptive pill which has enhanced women's sexual freedom stands accused of making them ill. Antibiotics which have helped to curb infectious diseases are now blamed for creating drug-resistant strains of bacteria. The modern farming methods which have made it possible to abolish hunger are branded as spreaders of disease.

Every new scientific and technical advance now tends to be discussed not in terms of its potential benefits for humanity, but in terms of its possible side-effects. Typically, the completion of the Channel Tunnel, one of the wonders of modern civil engineering, was greeted less with celebrations than with warnings about how foreign diseases, foreign terrorists and foreign armies might use the Chunnel to invade Britain. Every advance in the field of genetic engineering, which holds out the prospect of immense benefits for humanity, can expect to be met with warnings about the Frankenstein factor. Even the Internet, one area in which technological enthusiasm survives today, is often discussed only as a potential transmitter of pornography and political extremism.

The unwillingness to use what we already have for the good of humanity, and the tendency to retreat rather than press ahead, are not confined to scientific or technological matters. The spirit of caution now seems to infect every sphere of social, cultural and political activity. Many of the most basic and once unquestioned gains of the past two centuries are being rolled back. The very concepts of knowledge, truth and rationality are now called into question with the rise of relativism and the notion that different views are equally valid about everything from art and literature to mathematics and morality.

Democracy, the self-proclaimed founding principle of Western politics, is now under attack from influential forces on several fronts, as the climate of mistrust and uncertainty undermines faith in *'demos'*—the people. Every proposed change to the political or legal system today— from empowering judges to reforming the jury system—seems to mean moving the levers of control further away from popular accountability.

All kinds of scientific, social and political achievements which were once cherished by society are now coming under attack. Yet these achievements are the accumulated wealth of humanity. Many are worth defending in their own terms. Taken together, they add up to a rich resource which humanity has built up in the course of its long march from the caves to civilisation. See how far we have come along that road, and any notion that things are now worse than they have ever been appears simply ridiculous.

Contrary to the impression given by the doom-and-gloom mongers, people in the developed nations are now healthier and living longer than ever before. The improvements in lifespan in parts of the developing world, such as Asia and even Africa, are in some ways even more dramatic (see Chapter Two). Many of the features of life which are supposed to be deteriorating today have actually improved beyond recognition. The suggestion that modern farming methods make food less healthy than in the past ignores the transformation of the quality of food available over the past 20 years; go back a few years further and accounts of adulterated bread and rotten meat and vegetables were commonplace. Those who claim that Britain is becoming an increasingly violent society turn a blind eye to the facts about the unmatched brutality of life for working class people a century or even 50 years ago. Even the crusade against 'killer cars' misses the point that technical improvements mean deaths on the roads in the UK are now fewer than they have been at any time since records began in 1926. Of course, improvements in the human condition are not automatic or inevitable. But neither are disasters. What the current fatalistic approach to problems writes off is the *potential* for humanity to meet the challenges it faces. This argument will be explored in relation to various issues in the chapters that follow. But for now, let us take the question of the Earth's natural wealth, and the current preoccupation with the need to limit consumption in order to preserve what remains of the planet's depleted resources. Typically, this discussion of resources begins with a presumption of limits. It is assumed by the prophets of eco-doom, and accepted by many others, that the Earth has a fixed store of resources which are being run down by extravagant consumption. In fact, there is nothing fixed about the level of resources available.

Humanity has the capacity to replenish and restock many resources as we go. This is why, for instance, despite the continual wailing about mankind's murder of the planet's forests, there are more acres of forest land in America today than there were when Columbus came ashore in 1492. In any case, resources are not really 'natural' at all. Nature's raw materials are turned into productive resources by the intervention of human action. The more advanced the society, the more resources it is able to create from nature. Uranium or bauxite were not resources to primitive societies, which neither knew of their existence nor could have used them if they had. But, given the developments of modern science and technology, naturally occurring ores can be turned into highly productive resources. What is missing from the eco-doom scenario is any consideration of the way that human ingenuity can discover, develop and exploit new resources.

On this and many other issues, the capacity of people and societies to confront and overcome problems is underestimated by the most fashionably influential schools of thought today. It is not that the problems are greater, but that the will to resist and overcome them is weaker.

Despite the exaggeration of many dangers, and the tendency to label problems as insoluble even when this cannot be justified by evidence or argument, there are of course real problems in society: in particular, problems arising from exploitation and oppression. Yet the more real the problem, the more the mood seems to be one of acquiescence and acceptance. It is striking that those who promote scares about the perils of eating beef or passive smoking, have nothing to say about real problems like unemployment or poverty which blight the lives of millions.

There is today an unprecedented preparedness simply to live with the destructive consequences of capitalism. Unemployment is treated as a fact of life, a natural disaster beyond anybody's power to prevent. Many commentators not only accept the alienation that results from market forces, but even revel in it and the wider cult of the victim which has become so influential. What has changed most dramatically is not the experience of life's difficulties, but the spirit of acquiescence with which they are met. Every discussion appears to be about how to come to terms with a problem created by the profit-led system, rather than how we might overcome it.

For instance, there is nothing new about the problems of poverty and economic backwardness in the Third World. What is different today is that the contemporary discussion is not about how to end poverty, but how to adapt to it. The notion of 'sustainable development' is based on an acceptance that economic and social development in the Third World can only be limited. The argument for using only 'appropriate'—ie, primitive—technology in these societies reflects the view that the Third World has no alternative but to remain stuck in the industrial doldrums.

In Britain, it is a similar story with an issue like healthcare. There is nothing new about a shortage of funding for medical treatment, but what is new is the way in which public discussion now focuses, not on fighting the cuts or demanding more resources, but on deciding where the limits on treatment should be imposed. Thus there is now a major debate about 'ethical' rationing of healthcare, with influential voices arguing that those who fail to take proper care of themselves—like smokers—should be sent to the back of the queue for care. The argument is not about what we all need, but who deserves to receive treatment.

Discussions which focus on how to live with shortages and injustices, rather than on how to do something about the forces that give rise to the problems of society, are very much the order of the day. Yet there is so much more to be gained if only more people were prepared to raise their sights and set out to achieve their most ambitious aspirations. The trouble is that, today, too many people are too scared to realise the possibilities which already exist, never mind the potential for further gains.

If this situation is to change, a lot of responsibility rests with those who do have some faith in the potential of humanity to make tomorrow better than today. In an age when mainstream politics is dominated by the outlook of Tina—'There is no alternative'—we need to set a new agenda for now.

The precondition for developing an alternative agenda for change is to confront the sense of powerlessness which so afflicts people today, paralysing their ability to act. Until the notion that nothing in society can really be changed for the better has been challenged, caution and safety will remain the major preoccupations of society.

Our alternative needs to start by disposing of some of the myths that dominate public discussion. It is imperative to combat both the notion that we are beset on all sides by new and terrible risks that require us to take cover from modern life, and the attitude of acquiescence to the real problems that do confront us today.

A rational alternative needs to begin by raising the sights of society, and by refuting the damaging assumptions about the limits of what it is possible for people to achieve. Challenging the sense of powerlessness at every opportunity, and putting the case for the history-making potential of humanity, is the best way to counter the mood of caution and make an alternative realistic.

There may only be a minority today prepared to look at the big picture and stand up for change. But that minority is the key to questioning the conservative, cautious climate and to opening up the debate about the society in which we live and who controls it.

What we need now is to bring everything together in an alternative agenda that can influence discussion in a different direction as the political climate hots up around a general election campaign. We need an alternative explanation of how we got to where we are today, and more importantly, an alternative approach to the question of how we can move on.

'APOCALYPSE FROM NOW ON'

2

The inflation of the problems facing society
intensifies a sense of powerlessness and
appears to confirm the futility of any
attempt to change the way the world is.

That even an apocalypse can be made to seem part of the ordinary horizon of expectation constitutes an unparalleled violence that is being done to our sense of reality, to our humanity. (S Sontag, *AIDS and Its Metaphors,* 1991, (orig 1988), pp178-79)

In her perceptive commentary on the panic about AIDS in the late 1980s, the American critic Susan Sontag noted the widespread 'sense of cultural distress or failure' in Western society that seemed to create a 'need for an apocalyptic scenario' and 'fantasies of doom' (*AIDS and Its Metaphors,* p172). This gloomy mood explained the 'striking readiness of so many to envisage the most far-reaching of catastrophes'. Fears about an explosive epidemic of a lethal infectious disease compounded existing anxieties about the dangers of nuclear war, global warming and other environmental disasters, to create a peculiarly 'modern kind of apocalypse'. The end is believed to be nigh, but this is a protracted condition rather than a terminal event, a state which 'looms, but never happens'. It is a case, as Sontag puts it, not of 'Apocalypse Now', but of 'Apocalypse From Now On' (p173).

The sense of impending doom which Sontag detected in the 1980s has become even more pervasive in the 1990s, undoubtedly amplified by the imminent end of the millennium. AIDS has retained its status in the public mind as the modern equivalent of the plague, only to be joined by scares about new threats to health—such as Ebola and mad cow disease—and the reported re-emergence of old dangers, notably cholera, malaria, tuberculosis and diphtheria, often in drug-resistant forms.

Warnings of wider environmental disasters, resulting from unrestrained economic development, the exhaustion of natural resources, pollution and population growth have also grown more insistent, and more influential.

THE DANGER OF DOOMSDAY SCENARIOS

The prevailing *fin de siècle* pessimism is well summed up in the title of John Leslie's 1996 book, *The End of the World: The Science and Ethics of Human Extinction.* The opening pages list a series of problems which Leslie believes could shortly wipe out the human race. He includes nuclear war, plague, a supernova, a collision with an asteroid, even 'something-we-know-not-what' (p9). Leslie's grim prognosis has been challenged by some experts, but there can be little doubt that there is a wide resonance for his argument that humanity is in grave danger from a range of natural, social and technological factors. There is a growing consensus that human intervention has caused such far-reaching damage to the ecosystem that we are now merely waiting to find out the precise form of nature's revenge upon humanity.

There is a well-established perception that environmental issues now interact with political conflicts to produce uniquely explosive situations around the world. As one conservative American commentator puts it, the environment is '*The* national security issue of the early twenty-first century':

> The political and strategic impact of surging populations, spreading disease, deforestation and soil erosion, water depletion, air pollution,

and, possibly, rising sea levels in critical, overcrowded regions like the Nile Delta and Bangladesh, will be the core foreign political challenge....[A]n increasingly large number of people will be stuck in history, living in shanty towns where attempts to rise above poverty, cultural dysfunction, and ethnic strife will be doomed by a lack of water to drink, soil to till and space to survive in. (RD Kaplan, 'The coming anarchy', *Atlantic Monthly*, February 1994, pp46-77)

The spectres of environmental degradation and mass impoverishment now haunt the global imagination.

If the future forecast for poor countries sounds grim, there is little optimism either in the West, where concerns about the environment are compounded by a sense of social and moral decay. There is, for example, a morbid preoccupation in Britain with extreme manifestations of communal disintegration and personal depravity—such as the Rosemary West mass murder trial in 1995 and the Dunblane massacre in March 1996, and numerous other highly publicised instances of violence and abuse. The obsessive public discussion of these cases generally assumes that they provide insights into society at large, rather than seeing them as bizarre aberrations from normal behaviour.

The outlook articulated by the radical Real World Coalition in a manifesto published in early 1996 sums up the convergence of global environmental concerns with domestic preoccupations about social and family breakdown and individual insecurity:

For large numbers of people in Britain today, the new century is not a source of hope. The predominant mood, if anything, is of fear.

People are anxious about the future, about the world they are leaving for their children. They see, with a profound understanding quite missing from national political life, the growing crisis of humankind's impact on the environment, as the simultaneous growth of material consumption and population generates inexorably greater pollution and resource degradation. They witness poverty, famine and conflict in distant places and know that we cannot disclaim responsibility. They see the fabric of British society tearing under the strain of inequality and the glorification of me-first materialism. They foresee a world in which people live increasingly barricaded lives, fearful of others, besieged by crime; in which material wealth offers no substitute for the lost quality of community life. (*The Politics of the Real World,* p1)

The overwhelming nostalgia of popular culture, which endlessly recycles an increasingly homogenised past in diverse forms from pop music to televised costume dramas to the 'heritage' industry, reflects the mood of a society that has reached the end of the road and knows it. Numerous surveys report a deepening 'feelbad factor'. People look to the past with a sense of loss, regard their present existence as insecure and look to the future with apprehension. A Mori poll in April 1995 found that whereas 12 per cent of the population felt that today's children would inherit a better world than their own generation, 60 per cent thought that it would be worse. A Gallup poll suggested that some 63 per cent felt that children today faced a worse future than they had at the same age.

The public mood of fear about the future, uncertainty about

the present and nostalgia for the past poses dangers far more real than many of the supposed threats we face today. The notion that we are living in a state of 'Apocalypse from now on' undermines any aspiration to improve the world in which we actually live. If we are on the eve of destruction, then what is the point of trying to improve things? If we are in constant danger of extinction, then surely the best we can hope to do is to cling on to the world we know and attempt to put off the evil day, at least until tomorrow? As Sontag observes, it is no relief when the end fails to materialise as predicted (or when the inflated estimates of AIDS cases have to be scaled down by the public health scaremongers); we can only mutter our gratitude that our miserable existence has been prolonged for at least another day.

The inflation of the problems facing society intensifies a sense of powerlessness and appears to confirm the futility of any attempt to change the way the world is. It has the effect of lowering expectations and reconciling people to the limitations imposed by the existing state of society. It weakens the quest for solutions to real problems. In a society permanently on the verge of apocalypse, the zenith of human ambition can only be to reduce the risk of succumbing to a premature death.

The public preoccupation with threats to our collective or individual welfare has fostered a free-floating anxiety, which now exists in a heightened state of readiness to react to whatever danger, real or imagined, is identified next. This predisposition to see the worst in any situation is creating an obsession with avoiding risk—particularly the unknown and allegedly unknowable risks that may result from virtually any form of human activity, from breathing and walking in the sun to eating, drinking and having sex.

The result of the new risk-consciousness and the worship of caution is a climate of fear—fear of nature or the unknown, fear of other people, fear even of ourselves. The ultimate result is the systematic denigration of human achievement and, even more importantly, human potential, in society today. Science and technology and all forms of human intervention in the environment are now widely seen as part of the problem rather than as the potential solution. In short, the promotion of doomsday scenarios drastically restricts the scope of human intervention in the world, and so degrades the human potential for improvement and problem-solving.

Let us look at the tendency of modern society to exaggerate (or even invent) problems, by focusing on the upsurge of scares around three issues: epidemic diseases, crime and child abuse. These examples of the climate of fear well illustrate Sontag's point that 'an unparalleled violence' is being done both to our 'sense of reality' and to 'our humanity'.

FROM AIDS AWARENESS TO MAD COW MADNESS

In the decade since the Aids panic first swept the Western world we have experienced a series of scares about infectious diseases. Some have been associated with contaminated foods (eggs with salmonella, soft cheeses with listeria) and others have emerged from exotic foreign locations (such as the Ebola outbreak in Zaire). Others still are hardy perennials like meningitis, suddenly basking in the glare of publicity now guaranteed to lethal infections in an age that combines anxiety about disease and a ubiquitous mass media. The most recent large-scale public health scare in Britain erupted in March 1996 in response to the fear that beef infected with bovine spongiform encephalopathy (BSE) had led to cases of Creutzfeldt-Jakob disease (CJD) in humans.

The most striking common feature of these disease scares is the systematic exaggeration of the scale of the threat (see M Fitzpatrick, 'An epidemic of fear', *Living Marxism,* November 1995).

Take AIDS, the disease that has done most to foster the climate of fear and anxiety. AIDS is a terrible disease, but for the simple reason that HIV, its causative organism, is so difficult to transmit, it will never have the sort of catastrophic impact of the major epidemic diseases of the past. It is now clear that HIV has been present in humans for at least 20 years; it is 14 years since the first AIDS cases were identified in the USA. Amid all the wild speculations and exaggerated projections about the AIDS epidemic, the one hard fact is that it was not until late 1994 that the number of AIDS cases worldwide reported to the World Health Organisation (WHO) passed one million. No doubt that was an underestimate, though there are good grounds for suspecting that the WHO's 'guesstimate' of 4.5m cases is an exaggeration. According to the WHO itself, this figure emerges from a method that 'is only a form of collective educated guess and should be taken as such'.

Given that the eventual mortality from AIDS still approaches 100 per cent, this disease is undoubtedly causing an appalling loss of life. Yet, if we look at infectious disease in a wider historical context, there is no comparison between HIV and the great epidemic killers of the past. Take the plague organism itself. Yersinia pestis killed one third of the population of northern Europe in the four-year period between 1346 and 1350. Nor does HIV look so menacing alongside the influenza strain that killed 20m worldwide in the winter of 1918-19, more than the First World War itself.

But we do not need to return to the distant past to put AIDS in perspective. According to WHO figures published in 1991, 3.2m children below the age of five die every year in Third World countries from curable infectious diseases such as gastroenteritis, measles and whooping cough, exacerbated by malnutrition. Some 3.5m people still die every year from malaria, mainly in Africa. In 1970, before HIV became established in humans, three million people a year were still dying from tuberculosis. Even in Africa, AIDS is a long way from being the major threat to public health today. Old-fashioned poverty and squalor rather than exotic new viruses remain the biggest menace to humanity.

The much-hyped new viruses—Ebola, Lassa, Marburg and various other insect or rodent-borne bugs—are indeed highly lethal, but as many commentators have pointed out, this renders them less likely to cause an epidemic. They kill their victims too rapidly, before they have a chance to transmit the infection. Hence these viruses tend to cause small and short-lived outbreaks, affecting relatively few people. Many more people died invisibly in Zaire in 1995 from malaria, measles and diarrhoea than the 245 who succumbed to Ebola in the gaze of the world's media.

The novelty of these viruses, the dramatic illnesses they cause and the high mortality associated with them, make them well-suited to preying on and intensifying popular anxieties. In the case of AIDS, the cynical exaggeration of the risk of widespread HIV infection in the West, and the promotion of popular fears by diverse politicians, pressure groups and medical interests, has undoubtedly amplified public fears (see M Fitzpatrick and D Milligan, *The Truth about the AIDS Panic,* 1987). When we turn to some of the more recent scares—listeria, necrotising fasciitis, meningitis—we see a pattern of heightened awareness of relatively rare diseases in the absence of any evidence of a significant increase in incidence.

The increasingly irrational character of public concern about infectious disease found its most extreme manifestation so far in the great mad cow panic of March 1996 (see M Fitzpatrick, 'A mad, mad, mad, mad world', *Living Marxism,* February 1996; 'The great mad cow panic', *Living Marxism,* May 1996) Here, for the first time, was a panic about a disease which had not actually been shown to exist.

The hypothesis that BSE might be the cause of CJD is plausible: both are spongiform encephalopathies thought to be transmitted by 'prions'. But it is entirely unproven. There is not one case in which a human has been found to have contracted CJD through contact with 'mad cow disease'. Experiments conducted in the laboratory at St Mary's Hospital in London suggested that the agent responsible for BSE could not cross the 'species barrier' into humans (J Collinge, *Nature,* 21/28 December 1995). While the panic about BSE causing a CJD epidemic reached its peak, few seemed to notice the small fact that the overall incidence of CJD in Britain *fell* from 55 cases in 1994 to 29 cases in 1995.

In short the notion that BSE was the cause of CJD was a hypothesis for which there was only the weakest circumstantial support. Indeed there was considerable epidemiological and experimental evidence against it. Yet on 20 March 1996 health secretary Stephen Dorrell told parliament that the 'most likely' cause of the new cases of CJD was infection transmitted from cows with BSE. The result was a nationwide panic about the danger of contracting CJD from eating beef, a risk which may well be non-existent, is probably negligible and certainly unquantifiable. There followed a collapse in the demand for beef, a virtually worldwide ban on British beef exports, and a 'beef war' with Europe.

There was no hard evidence that BSE causes CJD. Yet the mad cow panic took hold at every level of society from the cabinet minister to the consumer, just as previous disease scares had apparently found many people ready to endorse the gloomiest worst-case scenario. The explanation for the wildly exaggerated public reaction can have little to do with the real facts about the particular health issue in question. Instead, the resonance for exaggerated disease scares reflects society's general predisposition to panic over alleged risks and potential dangers today.

One reason why the mad cow scare took off as it did was the automatic assumption among many commentators today that anything 'natural' is good, while anything 'unnatural' or man-made is suspect. There is growing support for the notion that new diseases like BSE, AIDS and Ebola are examples of the revenge of nature against human arrogance and interference. 'Is it altogether fanciful', asked the conservative Oxford philosopher John Gray rhetorically, 'to see the threat of a major outbreak of CJD as a symptom of nature's rebellion against human hubris? ('Nature bites back', *Guardian,* 26 March 1996). Intensive modern farming techniques—in particular, the feeding of animal protein to cattle—have been widely blamed for causing the problem. According to an editorial in the *Sunday Times,* 'nature has a habit of inflicting retribution on those who break its rules': 'natural herbivores have been turned into carnivores for the sake of improved farm productivity' ('Nature's revenge', *Sunday Times,* 17 December 1995). The *Guardian* agreed, arguing that 'the root cause' of BSE was 'intensive farming'; 'turning vegetarian animals into meat-eaters was asking for trouble' (*Guardian,* 8 December 1995).

These (altogether fanciful) views bear no relation to the real world or farming and agricultural science. Instead, they reflect modern society's extraordinary lack of confidence in itself. It is a simple fact that human civilisation is based on 'breaking the rules' of nature by cultivating plants and domesticating animals. The emergence of agriculture some 10 000 years ago was one of the first great triumphs of humanity over nature. Its intensive development has allowed humanity increasing autonomy from hunger and the arbitrary effects of the elements. Agriculture is by definition a violation of nature: there is no such thing as a 'natural' farming method. Modern cattle, for example, are the product of thousands of years of human intervention. Whether they are used

31

to produce milk or beef, they require a more nutritious diet than they would get simply wandering around a field. So-called organic farmers feed them clover or hay, perhaps supplemented with soya, silage and grain. For many years non-organic farmers have used feeds derived from fish or other animal sources.

There is little 'natural' about any aspect of the modern process of food production. It seems that the problem of BSE arose not from the practice of feeding cattle processed offal from sheep and other animals (according to the National Farmers Union, this has been done 'since time immemorial'), but from the recent relaxation of regulations governing the sterilisation of such animal proteins. In many ways the BSE story shows the effectiveness of modern methods of monitoring potential environmental hazards like this. A new technique was introduced, found to cause a new disease and banned—all within two years. As science writer John Gillott has observed, thanks to advances in science, 'the striking thing is that we face less of a "revenge of nature" problem today than we did in the past' ('Who's afraid of nature's revenge?', *Living Marxism*, May 1996).

The notion of the 'revenge of nature' continually over-emphasises the negative consequences and side-effects of human intervention in natural processes. Worse, it underestimates the capacity of contemporary science and technology to tackle whatever problems are thrown up by human manipulation of nature. A common feature of the exaggerated health panics of recent years is the irrational loss of faith in the potential of science to solve problems—a loss of faith which now even infects many within the scientific community itself.

The key development in triggering the mad cow panic was the shift in position of the experts in the government's Spongiform Encephalopathy Advisory Committee (Seac). Up to March 1996 this body had consistently responded to pressure from campaigners against modern farming techniques by insisting that there was no evidence to support the thesis that BSE posed a threat to humans. In March it suddenly changed its view and stated that BSE was the 'most likely' explanation for 10 atypical cases of CJD. It was not that there was any new evidence to justify this link, but simply that, as the experts could not explain the appearance of the new cases, they no longer had the confidence to dismiss the unsubstantiated BSE hypothesis. Instead they endorsed it, as various members of Seac speculated publicly on the possible size of the anticipated epidemic of CJD, which was soon dubbed in the media 'the human form of mad cow disease'.

One medical authority illustrates the trend. In an editorial in the *British Medical Journal* in March 1996, American public health expert Paul Brown recalled his judgement in a *BMJ* symposium on BSE/CJD in November 1995 that the available evidence suggested a 'negligible risk to humans', only to confess that 'it now appears that I was wrong' (30 March 1996). However, he adduced no new evidence to justify this remarkable about turn, but simply repeated the refrain that 'no better explanation is presently forthcoming'. Being unable to advance a better explanation for a hypothesis for which there is only the weakest circumstantial evidence is a dubious basis for endorsing that hypothesis. Yet, within a few sentences, Brown was raising the spectre of a 'potential medical catastrophe'. The fact that an eminent scientist can swing in four months from characterising BSE as a 'negligible risk' to warning of potential catastrophe on the basis of no new evidence at all indicates a disturbing instability and lack of conviction.

The scientific establishment and its paymasters in parliament all retreated in the face of the demand for conclusive proof that BSE does not cause CJD, which follows from the quest to eliminate risk, and was endlessly repeated by journalists and opposition politicians. Yet such a demand is absurd. The peculiar difficulty of having to prove that something does not cause something else arises from the presumption that some familiar activity—like eating beef, drinking, breathing—should now be assumed to be of lethal danger until proved otherwise. This is indeed a mad, sad world, in which all encounters with the natural environment are regarded as immanently life-threatening.

The successive panics about epidemics of infectious disease reveal little about the facts of the cases in question, but a lot about the modern tendency to denigrate humanity and to deny the human potential to improve things through intervention and invention. The message is that humanity with its scientific arrogance has messed up the Earth, and will get what it deserves by way of nature's revenge. As the American commentator Malcolm Gladwell has observed, the contemporary literature about the danger of new plagues exhibits a 'self-loathing' of humanity that goes far beyond the old Cold War images of the enemy as alien, beyond even Biblical notions of pestilence as punishment for wickedness ('The plague year: the unscientific origin of our obsession with viruses', *New Republic,* 17-24 July, 1995).

Take, for example, this passage from Richard Preston's thriller *The Hot Zone,* based on the arrival of the Ebola virus in the USA in 1989:

> The Earth is attempting to rid itself of an infection by the human parasite. Perhaps AIDS is the first step in a natural process of clearance. (1994, p367)

It seems that Preston and his co-thinkers take such a low view of humanity that they might almost welcome the new epidemics as a sort of purge.

In a similar anti-human spirit, Arno Karlen in his prize-winning work *Plague's Progress* draws a casual parallel between the aggressive behaviour and disease which results from overcrowding among rats and 'something similar' which 'seems to happen to other mammals, including humans' (1995, p121). He writes in positive terms of periodic mass 'die-offs' resulting from epidemics from the Middle Ages up to the Irish potato famine of the 1840s. A related feature of the plague literature is the attribution of human characteristics to microbes as these authors pay respect to their 'ingenuity' and 'cunning': the capacities forged through thousands of years of human civilisation are equated with those of a few strands of RNA/DNA.

What can we do to avoid disaster? For Laurie Garrett, author of one of the most influential accounts of impending viral Armageddon, 'ultimately, humanity will have to change its perspective on its place in Earth's ecology if the species hopes to stave off or survive the next plague' (*The Coming Plague: Newly Emerging Diseases in a World out of Balance,* 1995, p618). We must, in other words, cease our quest to advance and develop human civilisation and accept a more humble place in the natural order. We must respect microbes and conserve the biodiversity of the planet. We must curb human population and any industry or other human activity that might risk upsetting the planetary ecosystem. We must, above all, in the words of the distinguished medical historian William McNeill quoted by Garrett, be 'conscious of the limits upon our powers' (*The Coming Plague,* p6). The ultimate consequence of the exaggerated and invented health panics of our time can only be to endorse a culture of limits and restraint in every sphere of human activity. The irony is, of course, that, inasmuch as real threats to human health do exist today, the record suggests that our only real hope of overcoming them is to push forwards the enquiries and inventions of medical science.

THE RISE AND RISE OF CRIME

> When we talk about being tough on crime and tough on the causes of crime, it is a message warmly welcomed in housing estates across the land, where people, often trapped by poverty or unemployment, are tormented by criminal behaviour, anti-social or violent neighbours, and drugs. (T Blair, 'My vision for Britain', in G Radice (ed), *What Needs to Change: New Visions for Britain,* 1996, p8)

Crime has become a key theme for New Labour and there can be little doubt that Tony Blair's vision of a nation of people living in terror of crime strikes a popular chord. Blair's lieutenant, Peter Mandelson, who claims an instinctive feel for the mood of the people on this as on many other subjects, insists that 'for many people crime is now the number one social and political issue' (P Mandelson and R Liddle, *The Blair Revolution: Can New Labour Deliver?*, 1996, p132). Nor is he short on toughness: 'crime is wrong and deserves to be punished'. With a series of proposals, including coercive measures against 'aggressive begging' and 'squeegee merchants' and powers to evict noisy neighbours and round up children on the streets after dusk, New Labour has attempted to outflank the Conservatives, the traditional party of law and order.

The perception that crime has risen in scale and viciousness in recent years has acquired the status of an unquestioned assumption of public debate. But is it true? What does the widespread fear of crime and the fact that crime can emerge as a major political issue tell us about our society?

There are two major sources of statistics about crime that inform much of the public discussion. Police records of notifiable offences provide a basic index of criminal behaviour from the front line of the criminal justice system. Surveys based on systematic questionnaires conducted with members of the public provide an alternative source of information. The *British Crime Survey*, based on over 10 000 interviews conducted throughout England and Wales in 1992, complements the results of earlier local research projects, such as the *Islington Crime Survey*, and provides the most systematic information currently available about the experience of crime. The results from both sources—

and the differences between them—shed some light on the question of the changing incidence of crime and the way it is seen.

The record of notifiable offences certainly appears to confirm a dramatic rise in crime over the past half century, though it also suggests a slight decline since 1992. Between 1954 and 1992, the number of offences notified to the police increased from just over 0.5m to 5.4m. Since 1970 the average annual rate of increase has been five per cent, accelerating in the 1980s. These figures would seem to justify the judgement of the conservative commentator Digby Anderson that 'crime and disorder have soared over the past 50 years'. (*The Loss of Virtue,* p3)

However, as numerous commentators have noted, statistics of notifiable offences are subject to a range of influences, which have to be taken into account in interpreting these figures. The most obvious is that they depend on the way in which crime is defined. This means that they do not include many forms of behaviour which may cause serious losses, injuries, even the deaths of many people—for example, through major commercial fraud or the neglect of safety regulations in building and transport—but which are rarely recognised as crimes. Perhaps more significantly, the figures do include many forms of behaviour which are now seen as criminal offences, but would not always have been so.

The notion of what is a crime is not decided simply by a physical act. Crime always has a social definition, one which shifts according to circumstances. Most obviously, the act of killing a man might earn you a murder conviction in one set of circumstances, but a medal for valour in another. As society has become increasingly anxious, insecure and obsessed with safety and order in recent times, so the definitions of what constitutes criminal behaviour have become increasingly broad. The category of 'crime' now includes many things which might have been seen as acceptable or at least put up with in other times and places. (To take one slightly extreme example, the Criminal Justice Act of 1994 made it a crime to dance in a field to music with a repetitive beat.) The consequence of this redefinition of crime is often to amplify the sense that society is threatened by an upsurge of criminal acts. But it is important to bear in mind that what has changed most dramatically is not the reality of people's behaviour, but the way in which that behaviour is perceived by others.

In a more particular sense, the category of 'notifiable offences' as specified by the Home Office is itself subject to change. The introduction of the notifiable offence of 'criminal damage' in the early 1970s and the removal of the lower limit on the value of the damage caused before an offence could be recorded in 1977 both led to sharp increases in recorded crimes. Changes in recording procedures in the 1980s led to an increase in notifications of vandalism and violence and to a decrease in 'acquisitive' crime, though the overall level remained steady. Former *Times* editor Simon Jenkins has pointed out that recorded crime has increased steadily since figures were first collected in the 1830s, 'roughly in line with police employment':

Today some 60 per cent of recorded crime is by children under 18. The Children Acts of 1907 and 1933 brought thousands of children who previously had been at the mercy of local constables within the reach of the courts. Both acts led to "crime waves" that shocked the nation, but were wholly definitional. (*Against the Grain,* 1994, p83)

The most important influence on figures of notifiable offences is whether or not the experience of crime is reported to the police. Results from the *British Crime Survey* suggest that the major change that took place in the 1980s was an increasing readiness to report crimes: whereas 31 per cent of all claimed experiences of crime were reported in 1981, by 1991 the proportion was 43 per cent. This increase, accounting for much of the increase in the official crime figures of the 1980s, took place for both crimes against property and against the person.

Why were people more willing to report crime in the 1980s? The authors of the *BCS* suggests three reasons:

• Insurance: whereas in 1987 only 37 per cent of people were covered against theft and damage, by 1991 this had risen to 50 per cent. Insurance companies generally insist that offences are reported before claims can be made.

• Age: older people are more inclined to report crime and the population is ageing.

• Sensitivity: the sharpest increases in recorded crimes were for offences regarded as 'less serious', suggesting that an 'increased public sensitivity' to crime led to a greater tendency to notify the police. (p18)

A fourth reason is suggested by the marked increase in applications for awards from the Criminal Injuries Compensation Board, rising from 26 500 in 1981/82 to 61 400 in 1991/92. The increase was particularly dramatic after the 1988 Criminal Justice Act widened the criteria for awarding compensation (Home Office Research Department, *Digest 2: Information on the Criminal Justice System,* 1993, p21). Clearly the prospect of compensation increases the likelihood that an offence will be reported.

What then can we conclude from figures showing an increase in notifiable offences? Jenkins is candid:

> The first thing to say is the police statistics are almost totally useless, either as a true record of crime or as a measure of its movement over time. They are simply a record of police station activity. (*Against the Grain,* p81)

In contrast to police figures, the *British Crime Survey* (carried out for the Home Office by academic criminologists from the University of Glasgow in 1992 and due to be updated in 1996) offers another way of measuring crime. Based on interviews with a randomly sampled selection of the population, it records respondents' subjective experience of crime. The most striking result that emerges from this approach is that it suggests a level of crime between four and five times higher than that calculated from police records of notifiable offences—a total of 15m crimes in 1991. The gap between this subjective experience of crime and the official figures, has been dubbed by the authors of the *BCS* the 'dark figure' of unreported crime.

How can we make sense of the 'dark figure'? No doubt many factors contribute to it. Many thefts and burglaries, robberies and assaults go unreported because people reckon that the chances of the police apprehending the villain or recovering the property are so low as to make it not worth the effort of reporting the incident. Many victims of crime feel that going to the police might involve them in procedures which are at best time-consuming and at worst intimidating and humiliating. Much unreported crime, like much reported crime, is of a relatively minor character. It is also likely, given the fickle nature of human memory and perception of past events, that much unreported crime would not, when assessed by a disinterested party, come under the category of notifiable offences.

This is not to say that recording the subjective experience of crime is without value. It is simply to recognise that, as a useful marker of popular perceptions of the experience of criminal behaviour, it cannot be regarded as providing any objective evidence about changing levels of crime.

The problem with the *BCS* approach to crime is that, at a time when there is such a heightened sense of social malaise, it provides ready headlines about rising and unreported crime and ready confirmation of the widespread prejudice that our society is sinking into a slough of criminal depravity. The readiness of academic commentators to endorse this prejudice reinforces its influence. Take, for example, Oxford sociologist AH Halsey, a veteran commentator on social affairs. In the opening paragraph of his introduction to a 1993 Gallup survey of youth crime in Britain, he asks 'is crime a serious problem?', and immediately replies, 'in short the answer is *yes*'. The evidence? 'The Gallup survey shows that it is held to be an overwhelmingly serious problem by both adults and adolescents.' (*Youth Crime in Britain*, p3) But the fact that people believe crime to be a serious and growing problem does not prove that it is.

We can see the operation of a positive feedback mechanism in relation to crime. The high publicity accorded to the publication of crime statistics and their growing role in party political disputes, not to mention the vogue for televised reconstructions of crimes and the recruitment through the media of public assistance for police investigations, all have the effect of raising public anxiety about crime. This inevitably results in a greater tendency to report offences, either in surveys or to the police. Greater awareness of crime thus inexorably results in 'more crime', reported or unreported.

There is another indicator of crime that receives much less attention: the record of court convictions. This provides one measure of the outcome of the more serious type of offence over time that is less susceptible to the vagaries of police recording or public reporting. Of course it also has severe limitations: innocent people are regularly convicted and the guilty often go free, the tide of public opinion ebbs and flows in relation to particular offences, such as those arising in the context of football hooliganism, trade union militancy or domestic violence, undoubtedly influencing the deliberations of the criminal justice system.

Yet perhaps the main reason why there has been little discussion of the changing rate of criminal convictions is that in recent years these figures have shown a marked decline.

Whereas the *BCS* suggests an 88 per cent increase in burglaries in the early 1990s, statistics on burglary convictions show a fall from 65 700 in 1980 to 40 300 in 1993, a decline of more than one third (D Rose, *In the Name of the Law,* 1995, pp102-03). In other words, this one objectively verifiable guide to changes in criminal behaviour reveals, according to David Rose, that over the 1980s 'convictions have tumbled drastically for many types of offence'. These figures, which generally enter public discussion only from the side of those who believe they reveal the softness of the criminal justice system, in fact suggest that the assumption of a major and growing problem of crime is, to say the least, dubious.

We can conclude that perceptions of crime have little relation to reality. This is indeed occasionally acknowledged by authorities in the field. Home Office minister David Maclean, noting the fall in recorded crime in 1995 and in particular the very low level of the much-feared crime of robbery, commented that 'the fear of crime is in inverse relationship to the risk of crime' (*Daily Telegraph,* 27 March 1996). Another expert, former judge and chief inspector of prisons, Stephen Tumim, freely acknowledged the limitations of the figures:

> Statistics are more misleading here than with most subjects, and we do not frankly know, save for personal experience in the streets, if crime against the person is going up or down. However, whatever the figures, it affects all ages and classes, disturbs and ruins lives.' ('Crime and punishment', in G Radice (ed), *What Needs to Change,* 1996, p190)

Tumim's last sentence reveals all: 'whatever the figures', fear of crime is prevalent throughout society. In other words, crime itself is not the issue, it is the wider sense of insecurity in society that has made people susceptible to an exaggerated fear of crime.

In a society which many people experience as out of control and threatening, people become particularly sensitive to the behaviour of others. In this climate other people are more likely to be perceived as a threat or a danger than as potential colleague or friend. 'Stranger danger', an old slogan warning children against alien adults, has now been universalised. The promise to crack down on individuals who appear most out of control in society appears to hold out the promise of a more secure future for the rest. In reality, the irrational fear of crime can only intensify the fragmentation of society into millions of vulnerable, anxious individuals, and diminish our collective humanity.

THE CHILDREN WE DESERVE

Once upon a time—and it was not so long ago—childhood was regarded as an age of innocence, and children were celebrated as a source of pride and joy to their families. They were cherished by society at large as an expression of faith in the future. Not any longer. In recent years familiar public images of childhood include the battered bodies featured in reports of the latest child abuse case or on the posters of children's charities, or the blurred video film of two-year old Jamie Bulger being led away to a violent death at the hands of two 10-year olds. It seems that if ever the media is short of a report about child abuse, physical, sexual or Satanic, or when there is no current case of murder, rape or violent assault by one child on another, then it is necessary to remind the public once again of the crimes of Myra Hindley, who was convicted of murdering several young children some 30 years ago and is kept in prison as a permanent symbol of the evil that lurks in our midst.

Like the threat of the new plagues, the danger to children is everywhere, but everywhere invisible. Unlike the menacing viruses and bacteria, this threat does not come from without—usually from some foreign country—but from within the most basic unit of modern society, the family. Like the level of crime, the incidence of child abuse is impossible to quantify, but it is also universally believed to be high and rising.

Yet expert inquiries into different forms of child abuse have failed to substantiate any significant increase in recent years. For example, the inquiry into the events in Cleveland in 1987 (when more than 100 children were taken into council care following the diagnosis of sexual abuse) noted published claims that the proportion of children suffering abuse could be as high as 10 per cent or more. It commented that 'such figures depend on what is meant by sexual abuse' and concluded that 'there was before the inquiry no evidence to support' such claims (Lord Justice Butler Sloss, *Report of the Inquiry into Child Abuse in Cleveland,* 1987, p5).

In her study of alleged cases of Satanic abuse in Britain (defined as rites including torture and sexual abuse of children and adults, forced abortion and human sacrifice, cannibalism and bestiality), Professor Jean La Fontaine concluded that there was 'no evidence that these had taken place in any of the 84 cases studied' (*The Extent and Nature of Organised and Ritual Abuse,* 1994, p30). Given the scale of public concern about these cases, La Fontaine admitted that she had been 'absolutely amazed by the lack of evidence supporting the Satanic abuse scare' (quoted in S Hinchliffe, 'Satanic ridicule', *Living Marxism,* January 1995). Clearly Satanic abuse is the child abuse equivalent of the mad cow panic.

Like the great fear about crime, the panic about children cannot be allayed by mere facts. Take, for example, a recent book by child-rearing guru Penelope Leach which opens with a dramatic change of tone from the liberal approach which made her so popular in the 1970s. Shocked by recent reports of child abuse and child delinquency, she emphasises that we need to get to grips with a major social problem:

> Whatever the real scale and scope of the horrors perpetrated on or by children, there are not hundreds, not thousands, but millions more who are being failed by Western society and are failing it. (*Children First: What Society Must Do—and Is not Doing—for Children Today,* 1993, pxiii)

The theme—'don't bother me with figures, I know the enormity of the problem'—is characteristic of discussions of child abuse (and other problems of the 1990s). In a strikingly similar book, Rosalind Miles, makes a strikingly similar point:

> The prevalence of today's news stories about criminal children, abused children, children out of hand, however much they smack of

newspaper hype and moral panic, point to a genuine, growing and justified concern. (*The Children We Deserve: Love and Hate in the Making of the Family,* 1994, pxiii)

When pushed to explain the source of the problem of childhood, Miles rounds up the usual suspects—the loss of family values, the decline in education, permissiveness, feminism, the recession. Then she gets closer to the point, observing that 'childhood has become a metaphor for a country that is out of control':

> At a deeper level many sense a dark communal malaise, a breakdown in parental morale, a failure of the will. It is as if we had given up, as if we no longer believe we can bring up loving, kind, well-behaved children capable of cherishing us and all that we hold dear. (*The Children We Deserve,* p8)

A society that hates and fears its own children is indeed one that has lost faith in itself and its future. But are things really so bad?

THE DENIGRATION OF HUMANITY

One of the results of the exaggeration of the problems facing society is that many of the achievements of humanity are either ignored or questioned. Indeed there is a widespread conviction that it is the development of human civilisation, particularly the advance of science and technology, and the resulting subordination of the natural order to the demands of human society, that is the source of many of today's problems of environmental destruction and social disintegration. Further developments in the sphere of science and technology tend to be greeted with apprehension rather than celebration. So recent advances in genetics or organ transplantation, for example, are regarded as creating more problems than benefits for society.

Despair about modern society fosters a nostalgia for the past, a sentimental affinity for primitive societies and even the tendency to blur the distinction between humanity and the animal world. The cult of the primitive, an undercurrent in Western society for more than a century, has acquired mass appeal in recent years. This is confirmed by the success of Hollywood's promotion of the ethical superiority of the 'native American' in films like *Dances with Wolves* and *Pocahontas* and by the impact of campaigns to save the tribes of the Amazonian rainforest by pop stars such as Sting and the Body Shop's Anita Roddick. The nineteenth-century drive to bring Western civilisation and Christianity to the 'Dark Continent' and other colonial regions, and the twentieth-century concern to promote development and modernisation in these areas, has been succeeded at the close of the millennium by the sentiment that 'we have much to learn' from peoples considered to be untroubled by the deep sense of alienation of modern society. The fact that virtually nobody in the West seriously envisages the possibility of reverting to some form of Neolithic existence confirms the mythic character of modern primitivism as a retreat from any attempt to remake society along rational lines into the world of fantasy.

The elevation of the natural world, in particular the world of animals, on to a par with—if not into a relation of superiority to—human society is another manifestation of contemporary despair. One of the curiosities of the Christmas 1995 television schedule was the broadcast of a film exploring the backward prejudices of a medieval France in which a pig could be put on trial for murder on the same weekend as a serious debate among prominent academics and other authorities about whether human rights should be extended to gorillas, chimpanzees and other primates. The systematic deprecation of the unique features of humanity, of our capacity for rational thought, for innovation, for the application of science and technology in the cause of human progress has led us to the verge of a new Dark Ages. Blurring the distinctions between humans and even the highest primates means turning our backs on the achievements of human civilisation and renouncing the possibility of an even fuller achievement of the human potential in the future.

Like a person in the grip of clinical depression, modern society is obsessionally preoccupied with its most negative features and exhibits all the manifestations of a low sense of self-esteem. Yet if we look around at the world in which we live there are, despite all the problems, many instances of positive achievements and many more indications of the potential for further advance. Let's look at a few examples.

● Life expectancy

The very fact that Western society has become concerned about its ageing population partly reflects the huge progress that has been made in recent years in humanity's struggle against disease.

Since 1950 there has been a 17 per cent increase in life expectancy worldwide: this increase has been most spectacular in the poorer countries of Asia where it has reached 20 per cent (United Nations, *World Population Prospects,* 1990 Population Study No120, 1991 p28). Even in Africa, the continent most afflicted by the economic and social problems of the late twentieth century, life expectancy is now more than 50.

Infant mortality rates today in Africa, Asia and Latin America are half what they were in the 1950s (United Nations, *Mortality of Children under Age Five: World Estimates and Projections 1950-2025,* 1988). In Africa, at that time, one third of all children born did not live to see their fifth birthday; today the figure is less than 20 per cent. In Asia the rate of infant death has fallen from 25 per cent to five per cent over the same period (*Mortality of Children under Age Five*).

Television images of famine in Africa have contributed to a general impression of a continent in a state of utter destitution. Yet such famines are much more of a rarity today than in the past and they are invariably the result of political and military disruption rather than natural disasters or population pressures. In 1969 one in three people in the world faced hunger daily; in 1996 the proportion is one in five (L Brown *et al, The State of the World*, 1996, p78). This improvement is partly attributable to advances in the production of food, in particular to the spread of intensive farming techniques.

● Health

One of the main reasons for the decline in mortality is advances in the control and treatment of disease. Some of the causes of devastating epidemics in the past have now been eradicated (smallpox) or drastically reduced by vaccination campaigns and improvements in hygiene (polio, diphtheria, whooping cough, tetanus and typhoid). According to the WHO the proportion of the world's children vaccinated against tetanus increased from 28 per cent in 1981 to 83 per cent in 1990 and the figures for polio and measles are 'broadly similar' (T Unwin (ed), *Atlas of World Development,* p112).

At a time when the return or persistence of infectious disease is a major theme of public debate it is important to take a balanced view. As we have seen, malaria remains a major health problem around the world, particularly in Africa; however it is equally important not to lose sight of the fact that the number of reported cases has fallen dramatically in recent years and now stands at 15 per cent of the figure for 1983 (WHO, *Weekly Epidemiological Records,* No42, 21 October 1994). There has been much discussion about the increase in old-fashioned infectious diseases, notably diphtheria and tuberculosis, in the countries of the former Soviet Union and to some extent in the West, particularly among the poor and homeless. But the problem here is clearly the collapse or decline of formerly quite efficient public health services rather than any peculiar upsurge in virulence or difficulty in treatment (the problem of the emergence of strains of organisms resistant to antibiotics is another old problem that tends to be greatly exaggerated). There has been an increase in tuberculosis in Britain, but this is really a mere blip on the long curve of decline.

Though the 'modern epidemic' of heart disease is a major focus of 'health promotion', it is not widely known that death rates from lung and heart disease are half what they were 20 years ago (*Social Trends,* No 26, 1996, pp129-30). Death rates for the under-65s have also halved since 1951.

● Literacy

Despite the prevailing gloom about children and the conviction that educational standards are declining (another prejudice immune to refutation by facts), there is much evidence of improvement, at least at a global level. Even in Britain, the number of people with higher educational qualifications has more than doubled over the past 20 years (*Population Trends,* No79, Spring 1995, p37).

In the developing world the proportion of children attending primary school increased from less than half in 1960 to around three-quarters in 1990 (*Unesco Statistical Yearbook,* 1991, pp2-31). In the same period, the proportion of children continuing at school up to the age of 17 increased from 35 per cent to 47 per cent. The proportion entering higher education roughly doubled, from eight per cent to 15 per cent in the Third World, and from 17 per cent to 36 per cent in the West (*Population Trends,* No79, Spring 1995, p37). Illiteracy has correspondingly fallen from around 75 per cent of the people of the

Third World before 1926 to less than 20 per cent today (Unesco, *Compendium of Statistics on Illiteracy,* 1990).

● Environment

Though many people today are convinced that we are being choked and poisoned by pollution, there is much evidence of improvement. The pea-souper fogs that were part of the life of London—and caused the deaths of thousands as recently as the 1950s—are a thing of the past, and fish once again swim in the Thames. In many northern cities a combination of deindustriali-sation and smokeless fuels has opened up vistas that had been enveloped in a permanent grimy cloud for decades. In the USA, outputs of carbon monoxide, lead, sulphur oxides and volatile organic compounds have been falling steadily since the 1970s and the number of 'bad air days' in major cities is also rapidly declining (Council on Environmental Quality, 'Environmental quality', *22nd Annual Report,* 1992, pp273-77). The production of CFCs—blamed for causing holes in the ozone layer—has fallen by 77 per cent in six years (see *The State of the World,* 1996, p14).

In the prevailing climate of gloom, the environmental improve-ments resulting from human engineering projects tend to be neglected. For example, the Kansai airport in Japan's Osaka Bay, a huge man-made island created by dumping three mountains into the sea, is a triumph of design and technology. The Channel Tunnel has established a historic link between Britain and the European continent.

• Values

At a time when the inclination is to wallow in the dark side of humanity, it is worth emphasising what American radical commentator Murray Bookchin terms the 'higher ethical sensibility' of modern society (*Re-enchanting Humanity: A Defence of the Human Spirit against Anti-Humanism, Misanthropy, Mysticism and Primitivism,* 1995). The twentieth century has witnessed appalling atrocities and relapses into barbarism and genocide. Yet, though the scale of degradation experienced in modern mass society may have been greater than in earlier times, it is only in our era that such events would have been popularly regarded with moral opprobrium. Torture, slavery, the slaughter of defeated enemies— before the modern era such activities were generally considered legitimate and went without question. Autocracy, hierarchy, elitism were considered to be features of a natural order vested with divine authority. It is only with the emergence of modern society, with its concepts of democracy and equality that the possibility of progress and of the improvement of humanity in both a material and moral sense arises.

It is ironic that sentiments of moral revulsion against the evils of modern society are often accompanied by a tendency to repudiate the framework of rationality and purposeful intervention in nature and society that make a more truly human society possible.

What we need is a more balanced assessment of the state of society, one that rejects the gross exaggeration of problems and recognises what we have achieved. From this perspective we can

55

begin to see more clearly that the limits on human progress do not lie in nature, but in the way that society is organised.

THE EVASION OF REAL PROBLEMS

One of the worst aspects of the domination of public debate by the sort of issues we have discussed—the new epidemics, crime and child abuse—is that, to the extent that the problems are real rather than imaginary, there is very little anybody can do about them. We can speculate endlessly about whether the Ebola virus might mutate into a virulent airborne agent of a global die-off or about whether we might catch meningococcal meningitis on the bus. But, short of retreating into a plastic bubble with air-conditioning there is little we can do to avoid these terrifying eventualities (and, should we opt for the bubble, we should not underestimate the risk of radon toxicity). It is true that some people make a living by robbing other people, but apart from taking routine precautions, it is in practice beyond our capacity to prevent such behaviour without again resorting to the plastic bubble and ensuring it has a sound mortice lock and bars on the window (but don't forget the smoke alarm).

There can be no doubt that some children are brutalised by their parents and that other children brutalise one another, but short of installing a policeman in every household and play-ground, it is difficult to see any short-term solution to these problems. Of course an attempt to impose a solution along just such lines, with surveillance cameras and networks of child protection social workers and other professionals, has developed in parallel with the child abuse scare. This, like the burgeoning of the criminal justice system, with more and better-equipped police, and more and more people in prison, as a response to the crime panic, is an example of a solution that is in many ways worse than the problem it is designed to tackle. These solutions do nothing to prevent child abuse or crime, but as we shall investigate later, lead to the development of an intrusive and coercive system of state authority that extends into virtually every area of public and private life.

While debates rage about problems that are non-existent, not susceptible to any practical response or invite solutions that are not only useless, but threatening to civil liberties, other problems, that could be resolved by measures of public policy, are avoided and neglected. So, for instance, the permanence of mass unemployment has ceased to be a live political issue in the West. And while those of a liberal conscience might wring their hands over the exaggerated fears of starvation and plagues in the Third World, the real but rather more banal problems of everyday poverty and a lack of transport and communications infrastructures in those societies is accepted as a fact of life.

We live in a society that has become obsessed with non-problems or problems with no solutions, that is oblivious to real problems that could be solved through collective effort. The common theme behind contemporary preoccupations is that we have reached such a precarious state that any attempt to move forward risks even greater catastrophe. While individuals are exhorted to take individual responsibility for accepting the restraints supposedly imposed by the limits of nature on human

57

society, social problems are redefined as personal inadequacies. The result is a uniquely stagnant and morose society in which human enterprise and initiative is stultified. Let us now turn to interrogate this sense of paralysis further.

THE POLITICS OF PARALYSIS

3

The central feature of the life of
modern society is the diminished role of
subjectivity. The culture of limits ascribes
a minimal role to the subject, the active
agency of human intervention.

If this social order cannot make a virtue out of hope, it can try to make a virtue out of despair. (M Bookchin, *Re-enchanting Humanity* 1995, p175)

Margaret Thatcher's famous dictum that 'There is no alternative' —or Tina for short—has outlasted her by several years. People may not often use the phrase itself any more, but the sentiment it expresses has come to be accepted across the spectrum of British and Western politics. All of the mainstream parties now insist that the capitalist market is the only viable regulator of economic activity in modern society. When New Labour officially ditched Clause Four of the party constitution, its historic commitment to public ownership, at its 1995 conference, it set the seal on the party's endorsement of private enterprise and the market, a position adopted in practice much earlier. The absence of any serious challenge to this policy from within the Labour Party or from any other source has amply vindicated Thatcher's defiant promotion of Tina.

If there is no alternative policy to that dictated by the market, then, as the Marxist philosopher Istvan Meszaros points out, there is no space for political life.

If it is true, as they say, that *'there is no alternative'* to the structural determinations of the capital system in the 'real world', in that case the very idea of *causal interventions*—no matter how little or large— must be condemned as an absurdity. The only change admissible within such a vision of the world belongs to the type which concerns itself with some strictly limited negative *effects* but leaves their *causal foundation* ...completely unaffected....

61

Such wisdom continues to be uttered without any concern for how bleak it would be if this proposition were really true. It is much easier to resign oneself to the finality of the predicament asserted in this blindly deterministic political slogan of our times...than to devise the necessary challenge to it. (*Beyond Capital*, 1995, ppxiii-xv)

If it is true that 'you can't buck the market', then there is little point in advancing any competing visions of society or even alternative policy options. In these circumstances politics becomes mere administration, a technical, managerial function.

Against that backdrop, it is not surprising that political debate in Britain and indeed throughout the West has become so restricted in scope and so trivial in content. If government policy simply follows the dictates of the Treasury, then politicians are reduced to quibbling over marginal rates of income tax and to having heated debates about licenses for dangerous dogs, or the size of the National Lottery jackpot. Nor is it surprising that, with all parties acknowledging the supremacy of the market, it has become more and more difficult to discern any significant policy differences among them.

The contraction of the political sphere has been accompanied by a growing conviction that the scope of government action itself has been gravely restricted by developments in the world economy. Fashionable theories of 'globalisation' maintain that, as a result of the growing scale and technological integration of the world market, particular nation states have lost the capacity to control even relatively minor aspects of their domestic economies. The logical extension of this argument—that the state can no longer act as an effective instrument of policy innovation—provides powerful reinforcement to the philosophy of Tina. The thesis of the weak state suggests that not only is there no alternative to the market, but that the government cannot even implement the policy to which there is no alternative.

The philosophy of Tina has fostered a psychology of low expectations which has pervaded society. In a period when it suffers a chronic lack of dynamism in both the economy and the realm of ideas, Western capitalism cannot generate popular enthusiasm or even unambiguous approval for its continued existence. The system, and those who run it, survive, not by promoting any positive vision, but by suggesting that the negative features of capitalist society are in fact attributes of human nature. The limits which the system imposes in every field of human activity are then depicted as confirmation of human limitations in general. As a result, a profound sense of the limited scope of human endeavour prevails at all levels of modern society.

THE DECLINE OF SUBJECTIVITY*

The combined influence of Tina and the thesis of the weak state has helped to promote a powerful and unprecedented culture of 'anti-politics'. Some intellectuals and activists have celebrated the new mood of anti-politics as a healthy reaction against the

---

* This section is substantially derived from F Füredi, 'Rescuing the subject', *Living Marxism*, November 1995

63

corruption and aloofness of conventional politics. They interpret the declining popular influence of government and of parliament and the parliamentary parties as a positive step towards enhancing the power of extra-parliamentary lobbies and forces. They welcome the loss of prestige of mainstream politics as an encouragement to the growth of the more informal new social movements and campaigns of the marginalised.

In fact, the affirmation of anti-politics expresses a profoundly conservative outlook. It is not, as it sometimes appears, a rejection of particular parties and politicians, but an expression of a deeper conviction that politics as such is futile. The very idea that anybody could hope to achieve any positive results through political action is increasingly dismissed as naive or arrogant. Those who perceive some sort of radical impulse behind the rejection of politics ignore the fact that the flip side of anti-politics is the acceptance of the world as it is.

Anti-politics is not so much an impulse towards empowerment as a gesture of resignation. The renunciation of politics means rejecting the efficacy of human intervention in society. It calls into question the basic belief that people can organise themselves purposefully to achieve some particular end. Such a perspective belittles the potential of human action and denies the possibility of changing the world for the better. Anti-politics is another way of saying that positive change is a contradiction in terms.

The decline of politics is reflected in the intellectual currents of our time. In the 1980s the celebration of liberal free market principles could not be sustained in the face of continuing economic stagnation. The thoughts of Adam Smith, FA von Hayek and Milton Friedman were rapidly overshadowed by the parallel development of two schools of thought: neo-conservatism and postmodernism. While welcoming the defeat of radical alternatives to the market, neo-conservatives have warned about the dangers of excessive individualism and the breakdown of community and tradition. From this perspective, change—even Thatcherite change—could only make matters worse, and so it has proved. The project of neo-conservatism is to rebuild, restore and conserve the social fabric rent asunder by the ravages of unrestrained market forces during the Thatcher era.

Postmodernist theorists are also deeply disenchanted with the consequences of change, but they recognise that tradition cannot be restored. However, they also reject any attempt to make history, on the grounds that such an attempt could only make matters worse. Their reaction to 'modernity' takes the form of attacking the presumption of any 'human-centred' project, dismissing any faith in reason and progress as naive and rejecting political ideologies as mythical 'grand narratives'. For Bookchin, postmodernism is a weary and nihilistic outlook which has emerged in response to contemporary social and cultural fragmentation as 'a consolidating ideology that holds the mind captive to the social order in the very name of fragmentation and its alleged virtues' (*Re-enchanting Humanity,* p175) The postmodern criticism of human action has converged with neo-conservative trends to foster a climate inhospitable to any attempt to change the world or improve society.

These inherently conservative trends are not confined to political and academic circles. Everywhere, it seems, an intense awareness of the limits imposed by the environment is complemented by deep concern about the possible dangers and unforeseen consequences of any new initiative. Optimism about the possibilities offered by the Internet, for example, can quickly become swamped by worries about the growth of a global network for the distribution of child pornography or fascist and racist propaganda. The successes of the Human Genome Project, which bring the promise of methods of preventing or treating inherited disorders, provoke fears about potential abuses of genetic engineering and experimentation.

The feeling that we live in a society that is both beyond our control and increasingly unstable is experienced as a heightened consciousness of the risks that we encounter in everyday life. As we have seen in Chapter Two, we feel that we are at risk from the environment (above all from the consequences of human interference in the environment, provoking the 'revenge of nature'), from other people (crime, road rage, bullying, diverse forms of abuse) and, in a sense, from ourselves (unhealthy lifestyles, addictions).

A sense of low expectations converges with a heightened sense of risk to diminish our common humanity. The fear of taking risks leads to an acceptance of tighter limits on the scope of human activity. The acceptance of such limits can easily turn into criticism of any human-centred worldview. Anybody who today upholds the benefits of science and technology for human society is likely to be condemned for an irresponsible lack of concern for the planetary ecosystem. In a similar way, anybody who affirms the superiority of human reason over animal instinct risks being accused of 'speciesism'. The denigration of humanity and the repudiation of the humanistic outlook that has been such a central feature of the development of modern civilisation is the logical outcome of contemporary political and intellectual trends.

The central feature of the life of modern society is the diminished role of *subjectivity*. The culture of limits ascribes a minimal role to the subject, the active agency of human intervention. Those who complain about the triumph of selfish egotism over solidarity today miss the key trend: the demise of old collectivities —trade unions, local communities, mass parties and political associations—has not led to the emergence of a dynamic individualism. Though politicians and commentators pay lip-service to the importance of the individual, a more influential theme of the 1990s has been the denunciation of the hedonistic and acquisitive values of the 1980s (now blamed for what are regarded as the 'excesses' of the Thatcher/Reagan era), and the promotion of a new ethic of community and mutual concern. Far from liberating the individual, the decline of collective organisation has only created a greater sense of isolation, powerlessness and vulnerability. As a result, both collective and individual action are now called into question.

The exhaustion of politics and the culture of limits restrict the scope for individual initiative. Few in society today aspire to extend the range of human possibilities—indeed such notions are widely regarded as futile if not dangerous. For most, survival is the zenith of personal ambition given the prevailing cultural and intellectual influences. The heroes of our self-pitying society are not those who have achieved something, but those who have suffered and survived, for whom Princess Diana is a sort of patron saint (see M Hume, 'All you need is love?', *Living Marxism*, January 1996). The emphasis on individuals as victims of circumstances rather than as makers of their own destiny continually minimises the role of the subject in society. The fashionable attack on masculinity is another aspect of this process: a caricature of male arrogance and violence is used to demean any activism or aggression or attempt to take control of affairs, and to elevate instead the values of passivity, docility and acquiescence to the status quo (see M Hume, 'What's wrong with masculinity?', *Living Marxism*, May 1996).

The degradation of subjectivity in a society that has traditionally placed the highest value on the rugged individualism of the entrepreneur is a sure sign of a deep-seated malaise in capitalist society. The roots of this malaise are to be found in a combination of economic stagnation and political exhaustion, leading to social paralysis.

THE CAPITALIST IMPASSE

Capitalist stagnation has now been a fact of life for two decades. Neither the periodic upturns nor the spectacular development of computer and information technology can compensate for the narrow foundations on which economic expansion has taken place. The stagnation of productive employment in the West reflects the inability of the system to absorb the creative powers of humanity.

Any market economy must expand if it is to survive. But in every developed industrialised economy over the past quarter of a century growth rates have slowed. In Britain the increases in national output, investment and productivity have been less than two-thirds the rates of the previous quarter century (see A Maddison, *Dynamic Forces in Capitalist Development*, 1991). This marks the second slump of the twentieth century, though it has proved less volatile and more protracted than the previous slump in the early 1930s.

The persistent decline in the dynamic of British economic growth since 1973 has resulted in serious long-term damage to society. In industry underinvestment has meant that capital stock has aged, from an average of around 10 years in 1973 to more than 12 years in the late 1980s (*Dynamic Forces in Capitalist Development*, p143). Even during the recovery phase in the 1980s it took until 1988 for real gross manufacturing investment to exceed the previous peak in 1979. By 1991 it was back below the 1979 level, where it has subsequently remained. As a result, net manufacturing investment—which takes into account the depreciation of existing capital stock—has gone into the red since 1992.

Overall fixed investment has been well below the levels traditionally recorded in a period of economic 'recovery'. At the end of 1995 business investment was only marginally higher in real terms than it was at the trough of the recession in the second quarter of 1992. This was in marked contrast to the experience of the previous two recessions, when business investment recovered quite rapidly. One of the most conspicuous manifestations of national economic stagnation is the decay of the infrastructure. The transport system in particular reveals the strains resulting from years of underinvestment. The dilapidated state of schools, hospitals and local government buildings testifies to the wider decay of the system.

Living standards have grown much more slowly than in the postwar decades and many on below average earnings have experienced no improvement or, in some cases, a slight deterioration. There has been a steady haemorrhage of 'real jobs' in permanent full-time employment. Though the total number of people in work has remained fairly steady, some 3.5m full-time jobs have been replaced by two million part-timers, more than one million more are self-employed and a few hundred thousand are in no-hope government training schemes. In the 1990s there has been a significant shift from permanent to temporary employment.

These employment trends are no longer due to the shift from manufacturing to services as they largely were in the 1980s, when a dramatic rise in part-time jobs for women in services occurred in parallel with a drop in full-time male employment in manufacturing. In the 1990s inferior 'flexible' employment is spreading throughout the economy and the 'feminisation of work' leads to deteriorating conditions for everybody. Whereas in the past women have accounted for 85 per cent of part-time work, half the part-time jobs created since 1993 have gone to men. Men also now take up most of the temporary jobs, which are spreading rapidly in some areas of manufacturing, notably engineering, and the metals, minerals and chemicals sectors.

Management guru Charles Handy has warned that 'to have a full-time job in an organisation will soon be the minority occupation' (*Independent*, 29 November 1995). He advises people to abandon the futile quest for a career and suggests that instead they should aim to build up a personal portfolio of temporary employers. In a society that has lost confidence in the future, the concept of a 'job for life' evokes only nostalgia for the past.

It is now widely recognised that the weakness of the British economy is chronic and profound. Despite all the efforts of government ministers to talk up recent signs of improvement, the 'feelgood factor' has proved elusive. Indeed the sense of capitalist impasse is widely shared today, with the result that people often perceive that their living standards have deteriorated even further than statistical indicators would suggest. They also experience their jobs and the wider state of the labour market as even more insecure than the statistics show. The perception of deterioration in all aspects of national life amplifies a 'feelbad factor' defying the best efforts of the government's public relations and news management experts. Even among apologists for the system, the demise of economic theory and the acceptance of slower growth rates signify the universally gloomy outlook.

The capitalist impasse is not just experienced in the economy, but infects every area of political and intellectual life.

It is paradoxical that the victory of the West over the Soviet system at the close of the Cold War only appears to have helped to accelerate the disintegration of intellectual commitment to the capitalist system. In his influential thesis that, with the triumph of liberal democracy over Soviet communism, we had reached 'the end of history', the conservative American commentator Francis Fukuyama predicted the demise of all alternatives to capitalism ('The end of history', *The National Interest,* No16, 1989).

Yet within five years, we saw not only the demise of alternatives, but the collapse of faith in free market capitalism as well. How are we to understand this paradox?

It is important to recall that the triumph of the West over the Soviet bloc, and of Western capitalism over the left and the labour movements at home, was the outcome of many decades of struggle. It is not so long ago that the Soviet Union was still regarded as a 'superpower', and, until well into the 1970s and even the 1980s, the trade unions and socialist parties were still an important political movement in many Western countries, including Britain. The defeat of all these forces was the outcome of long and often bitter conflict, which required the mobilisation of all the political and material resources of the capitalist system.

It is now clear that the process which led to the defeat of the old working class movements did not leave the ruling elite itself untouched. In fighting this class war, the leaders of capitalism were forced to undermine the intellectual foundations of their own system, and ended up losing confidence in their own project. The crusade against socialism meant invalidating many of the ideas associated with any conception of human advance or social progress. It is as though the difficulty of containing the subversive potential of the Russian Revolution of 1917 required the Western elites also to question retrospectively the values of the French Revolution of 1789. But these values—of respect for science and rationality as well as commitment to liberty and equality— were crucial to the emergence of the capitalist system in Europe in the nineteenth century and to its continuing legitimacy in the twentieth.

In vanquishing the advocates of fundamental social change, the champions of capitalism were forced to weaken the case for change of any sort. It is difficult to over-emphasise the demoralising, almost self-destructive character of this idea for a system which, in its heyday, effected the most dynamic process of social change in human history. This is truly Tina's heart of darkness: it is revealed as not only a repudiation of socialism and communism, but also as a *de facto* recognition that the capitalist system too has reached the end of the road.

Crushing a belief in even the possibility of rational social reform, never mind the potential of people to make history through political action, meant destroying any idea that human intervention could improve the world. The influence of such bleakly anti-human sentiments has disoriented many intellectuals: they are rendered incapable of mounting a coherent defence of the system or of projecting any positive vision of the future. They now uphold the capitalist order, not by promoting principles, but by eschewing any fixed positions at all. The message is: 'if we have nothing to believe in, then it because there is nothing worth believing in.'

Of course, any technologically advanced industrial society requires the application of science and reason in its day-to-day operation. Whatever the status of the concept of progress in its universities, capitalist society requires efficiency and effectiveness in its factories and offices. Despite the intellectual crisis, entrepreneurs attempt, as far as possible, to carry on business as usual. The result is a paradoxical relationship between the theory and practice of capitalist society: at the same time we have intellectual stasis and technological development alongside one another. One of the central features of the contemporary crisis of society is that, though practical activity and innovation continue, they do so in a climate of unprecedented intellectual diffidence and self-doubt. A lack of faith in the efficacy of human intervention has become widespread in modern society.

The loss of confidence of capitalist society is most strikingly revealed at the level of the business enterprise. It is ironic that the capitalists themselves, who so recently emerged triumphant from the Cold War, should feel so insecure about their position. Yet it has become a commonplace that business managers have become scared to manage. As many of them seek to pass the responsibility for the most elementary decisions to specialist advisers and consultants, a veritable industry of management training and consultancy has come into existence. When directors encounter difficulties, their first thought is to call in a public relations expert to advise them on the niceties of 'ethical' management.

The loss of nerve of authorities in every sphere of society—in the private and the public sectors, in industry and services, in the professions—has led to the proliferation of new rituals which help them to avoid problems and put off confrontations. Many institutions now rely on 'facilitators' or 'consultants', 'mentors' or 'counsellors' to help to contain the tensions and conflicts that inevitably arise from the struggle to survive (let alone prosper) in today's straitened economic circumstances. In an attempt to compensate for the lack of a sense of direction, they draw up 'mission statements', 'codes of conduct' and 'charters'. Yet the very need for such documents only indicates that the institution concerned has no clear mission or purpose. In this climate the mere mention of the traditional rugged capitalist entrepreneur is enough to provoke acute anxiety attacks among managers whose claim to authority is a parchment certifying their MBA.

A similar pattern is apparent among scientists. For example, those engaged on research in the areas of genetics and assisted reproduction are increasingly reluctant to take responsibility for their own actions, preferring to invite some external agency to regulate their work. In many areas of clinical medicine, decisions once taken by doctors in consultation with their patients are now referred to ethical committees, or even to the courts and the media.

In the realm of aesthetics and culture ambivalence and indeterminacy are even further advanced and often enthusiastically endorsed. A promiscuous relativism, the conviction that no point of view can be considered better than any other, competes with a fashionable primitivism, the rejection of technological and social advance in favour of the ancient and aboriginal.

The general failure of nerve encourages an evasion of responsibility at every level of society. Just as managers are afraid to manage, so teachers often seem reluctant to teach and parents appear unsure how to rear their children (see M Fitzpatrick 'The problem of parenting', *Living Marxism,* June 1996). The emergence of counselling, help lines and other forms of professional intervention in everyday life are expressions of the prevailing sense of helplessness which also do much to reinforce it (see B Adams, 'The counselling con', *Living Marxism,* March 1994). The diminishing of subjectivity, the limiting of the scope for human action, encourages a state of affairs in which apologies and excuses can become the norm.

THE WEAKENING OF SOLIDARITY

It seems that everybody, whatever position they occupy, experiences the impasse of capitalist society in a highly individualised way. This may take different forms for a company director and a casual worker, a shop owner and a shop worker, a hospital consultant and a porter, but they all appear to feel an increased sense of personal insecurity at work, at home, in society at large. In drawing a contrast between the depression of the 1930s and today's slump, Simon Head offers a valuable insight into this phenomenon:

> Today, as in the 1930s, the market is creating more losers than winners. But 60 years ago the divisions among workers, managers and owners were much clearer, and entire categories of workers could not be displaced so quickly by new technology. Today the distinction between winners and losers and its causes is less well understood. ('The new, ruthless, economy', *New York Review of Books,* 29 February 1996)

The divisions were clearer in the 1930s because it was then easier to identify distinct classes with distinctive modes of thinking and acting, which were often in clear conflict with one another.

Different social classes were more visible in the past because they were given a clear shape by organisations and institutions which provided them with coherence and a collective identity. It is the demise of these bodies in recent years which has ensured that the slump of the 1990s is experienced in ways which are intensely personal, individuated and disorienting. This is most apparent on the side of the working class, but it has also become a major feature of other sections of society.

The trade unions have been effectively destroyed as collective organisations of the working class over the past two decades. Official membership figures have declined from the 1979 peak of 13m to under seven million in 1996. Trade unions have more members in the declining manufacturing industries and public services than in the more dynamic high technology, financial and private service sectors.

But the demise of the trade union movement is not simply a matter of falling membership rolls. More important is the transformation in the function of trade unions. Figures for strikes and other forms of industrial action over jobs and pay have been running at historic lows for several years, and even on the rare occasions when strikes do occur they tend to be short-lived tokenistic efforts which often have the character of 'going through the motions'. Where trade unions have survived in the workplace, they are usually to be found fulfilling the functions of junior personnel management. Outside the workplace, trade unions' main concern is often with providing various personal financial and other services to their members. These organisations are trade unions in name alone.

The Labour Party's links with the working class were traditionally maintained through trade union affiliation. This has been drastically curtailed in recent years, a process accelerated by the introduction of the 'one member, one vote' reforms under Tony Blair. Though often presented as measures to make Labour more democratic, in practice they have been used to enhance the power of the leadership—note, for example, the imposition of women-only shortlists and other favoured candidates at the discretion of the leadership. Disputed selection procedures in Leeds, Swindon, Birmingham and East London all confirm that New Labour's leaders will make sure that the party has MPs who are middle class and middle of the road.

Under Blair, Labour claims a dramatic rise in membership, from 270 000 to 350 000, though this remains a long way short of the 1952 peak of more than a million members. More striking is the fact that New Labour is now an overwhelmingly middle class party, with 49 per cent of members drawn from the 'salariat' and 57 per cent living in households earning more than £20 000 a year ('Official: Labour is middle class', *Sunday Times,* 7 April 1996). The average age of Labour Party members is 43.

Furthermore, the relationship between New Labour and its members is fundamentally different from that of a traditional social democratic party which was always, at least formally, committed to providing a collective voice for its working class members. While the process of New Labour policy formation by cabal has been widely discussed, the exclusion of the grassroots membership has passed without much comment. Yet in his recent book Peter Mandelson explains that in New Labour 'debate and political education' take precedence over the 'resolution-based politics' of the past:

> Instead of activity dominated by meetings, minutes and agendas, constituencies undertake campaigning, education and socialising, which are more interesting and stimulating for old and new members alike. (*The Blair Revolution,* 1996, p215)

This sort of activity is no doubt particularly stimulating for leading figures like Mandelson, who can dictate the nature of the campaigning, decide the content of the education and even pop in for a bit of socialising—all without having to face any of the awkward questions that might come up at meetings at which members have a right to decide on agenda items, vote on motions, and use the minutes to hold officers to account for decisions taken at previous meetings.

While the trade unions have been crushed by the cumulative impact of more than 20 years of mass unemployment and defeated strikes, and while New Labour has devoted itself to the quest for middle class respectability, the working class has lost cohesion. The parallel demise of other institutions has contributed to the collapse of the labour movement. The Communist Party and the left, which provided a network and a wider identity for generations of militants, finally disintegrated with the fall of the Soviet Union. Local organisations which once provided a focus for activists—trades councils, miners' institutes, clubs and libraries—are either defunct or serve an exclusively social function.

The breakdown of a labour movement which played such a key role in the life of the working class—and in many ways in the life of the wider society—has inevitably contributed to the experience of atomisation and the sense of vulnerability resulting from the slump.

The disappearance of the working class as a political force might be presumed to be a source of triumphal celebration for capitalism. But the ruling elite also has problems of its own. In the absence of a dynamic economy, tendencies towards fragmentation and conflict within the British establishment have become more conspicuous and more damaging. Ironically, the defeat of the labour movement and the collapse of the Soviet Union have added to this process of fragmentation at the top of society, by removing the old enemies against whom the capitalists could always unite in the past.

One of the most troubling problems for the British establishment of late has been the declining prestige of some of its most treasured institutions. The welter of marital strife and scandal surrounding the monarchy has led to a widespread questioning of its role. The Church of England increasingly appears either anachronistic or absurd, and often both. The BBC and the Civil Service have been ravaged by market forces and rancorous internal conflicts. One of the most telling indicators of the demoralisation of the establishment is the willingness of everybody from former cabinet ministers to the former lovers or domestic servants of members of the royal family to trade loyalty for a substantial advance from the publisher of their tell-tale memoirs.

The state of internal strife and division in the Conservative Party, in many ways the most successful political party in the Western world through the twentieth century, reflects the wider tensions within the British ruling classes and their middle class supporters. The most conspicuous axis of conflict is over Europe, but this is largely because it provides a focus for the expression of concerns about sovereignty and national identity which arise closer to home. The party whose formal title is still 'Conservative and Unionist' has long since broken its historic links with Ulster Unionism and it clings on to only a handful of seats in Scotland and Wales. Its base in local government in major urban areas has been shattered as the party has been driven back further and further into suburban and rural England.

The apparently inexorable slide of Tory fortunes in the opinion polls since John Major's 1992 election victory, and the party's unremittingly disastrous performance at by-elections, are well known. The leadership election spat between Major and John Redwood in the summer of 1995, though decisively won by Major, brought to the fore the extent and bitterness of the party divisions. The party's declining membership reveals members voting with their feet after the ultimate disappointment of the promise of Thatcherism. The party that claimed three million members in the 1950s is now down to 756 000 and is losing 64 000 a year: their average age is 66. Political scientist Paul Whiteley and his colleagues estimate that active membership is down to about 165 000 and that 17 per cent of members have stopped being active over the past five years, suggesting a '"de-energising" of the grass roots over time'. (*True Blues: The Politics of Conservative Party Membership*, 1995, p69)

Other surveys suggest that, while many working class voters won over to the Tories by Margaret Thatcher drifted away after Major's election win in 1992, middle class supporters have also started to defect. According to Gallup, in April 1994, a 20 per cent fall in support for the Conservatives among voters classed as ABC1 over the previous two years had given Labour a small lead in this influential constituency. Another poll revealed that only 13 per cent of ABC1 voters would trust a Tory politician.

The crisis of the Conservative Party as the party of the British establishment, as Britain's true 'natural party of government' and as the mass party of the middle classes reflects the profundity of the problems facing British capitalism. Given the party's preoccupation with managing its internal squabbles and its haemorrhage of support, not to mention its associated financial problems (and the aura of sleaze and corruption surrounding them), the Conservative Party can do little to provide a more cohesive front for beleaguered British capitalists.

There is a widespread tendency to underestimate the scale of the changes beneath the surface of British politics. The fact that the same parties (largely) still exist and many of the same faces are still around (for example, Arthur Scargill can still be seen at the TUC congress, Tony Benn at Labour Party conference, and the Normans Tebbit and Lamont at Tory Party events) reassures those who cling to continuities with the past. Even those who recognise, for example, the profound differences between trade unions like Unison in the 1990s and Nupe in the 1970s, or between New Labour and Old Labour, often expect that things will eventually 'return to normal' and the old patterns will reassert themselves. The threat of a strike in the public sector is still regarded as a harbinger of a new 'winter of discontent' (the season may be varied as circumstances require) along the lines of 1978-79. Shifts in opinion polls are interpreted according to the 'swingometer' model devised by the election commentator Robert Mackenzie in the 1960s. More radical commentators place special hope in some swing of the pendulum of political fortune back from right to left; the longer they have to wait the more fervent their sense of anticipation—and the more certain their eventual disappointment.

Unfortunately for those who would prefer to return to the safe certainties of the past, it is not possible to gain real insights into today's world by using the old models. The clock is not going to run backwards and the battles of yesteryear are not going to come round again. While the rump of the old Labour left dreams of a rerun of its great victory in the 1945 election, and the remnants of the Thatcherite right hope for a return to the triumphs of the eighties, the real world has moved on. Those of us who want to have a say in the future have to come to terms with the changes in the present.

It is not that everything has changed—there are always elements of continuity with the past. What has changed most are public perceptions of reality—in particular, the perception that Tina now rules—which creates the impression of a wide gulf between the present and the past. But this impression is very important. It is enough that people believe in the limitations on what human action can achieve today for human action indeed to be limited. In these circumstances, types of activity that in the past could have made a difference, such as going on strike, a protest demonstration or supporting a mainstream opposition party, can acquire a purely token character.

BEYOND LEFT AND RIGHT

The embrace of Tina and the consciousness of limits by mainstream movements of left and right has led to a pragmatic conviction that it is only worth attempting what appears to be realistically possible, and that there is no point in taking risks. Both left and right elevate expediency over principle, putting the highest value on narrow electoral considerations. The result is a uniquely depoliticised culture in which all sides avoid debate over principle or indeed any real clash of views. Modern politics is characterised by a convergence of left and right which makes the very use of these well-established labels pretty meaningless.

The fear of taking a stand leads directly or indirectly towards a relativist outlook which condemns any expression of principle as extremist or fundamentalist, and fosters a climate of opinion in which any statement of conviction is considered illegitimate.

Inside Blair's New Labour, declarations of lack of principle have become a clear indication of a rising career. Every week seems to bring another statement by a New Labour politician either pouring scorn on some traditional position of the Labour Party (for example, support for comprehensive education, opposition to the Prevention of Terrorism Act) or attempting to take up some traditional policy of the Tories (on welfare or law and order). Yet the Conservative Party is equally spineless. For John Major it is a matter of principle that taxes and public expenditure should be cut, yet his government has increased both.

One issue that reveals the way the major parties have moved closer and closer together to occupy a smaller and smaller political space is that of taxation. Tax has been a major focus of controversy in recent elections—indeed it is widely believed to have cost Labour the 1992 election—and is likely to figure in the forthcoming contest.

Though John Major claims that the Conservatives are by instinct a party of low taxation, his government has bitterly disappointed its supporters by imposing higher taxes, especially on the middle classes, in the form of freezes on the higher rate of tax threshold, cuts in mortgage tax relief and in the married couples tax allowance. In its campaign, the Labour Party is determined to make the most of the Tories' discomfort, promising billboard posters featuring the gigantic hands of a Tory chancellor wringing the poor taxpayer dry. However, Labour, as the party traditionally associated with public expenditure financed through progressive taxation, still feels vulnerable. When shadow cabinet member Clare Short appeared to suggest in April 1996 that middle income families ought to pay 'a bit' more tax, she was promptly silenced by Blair's spin doctors.

On the other hand, Paddy Ashdown's Liberal Democrats have openly paraded their policy of increasing income tax to pay more for education. In the Littleborough and Saddleworth by-election in 1995 the Labour candidate, with Peter Mandelson at his elbow, denounced the Liberal Democrat as a champion of high taxation. Though the Liberal Democrat won, Mandelson's opportunist tactics marked a new departure for New Labour, one that is likely to reappear in a bid to excite the public at the forthcoming general election.

The great debate about tax reveals how narrow the terms of political debate have become. The general level of taxation in Britain is relatively low by European standards (though higher than in Japan or the USA) and, for people on average earnings, has not risen much in recent years. According to journalist Peter Kellner, only 1.5m people fall into the income group (£28 000 to £45 000 a year) most affected by the recent changes

(*Sunday Times,* 27 March 1994). It is not that the issue of tax has got bigger, but that the other issues appear to have got smaller.

In the past, elections have turned on the question of the distribution of income across the whole of society, as incomes policies, economic plans and welfare programmes have been put before the electorate. Though these discussions of how best to build a dynamic economy and abolish unemployment and poverty promised more than they delivered, they provided at least the semblance of a national debate about competing visions of a more prosperous future. But no party has such a vision today in an age of stagnation and lowered expectations.

Various government measures in the 1980s, including the privatisation of the public sector, the devolution of pay bargaining to company or workplace level and the general retreat of the state from welfare provision, have effectively removed the determination of income from the sphere of politics (while anti-union laws have strengthened the hands of employers in pay bargaining). Now that important matters affecting living standards have been pushed off the political agenda—usually by measures endorsed by New Labour—there is little left to discuss apart from tax levels. Furthermore, people who might once have hoped to negotiate a better pay deal through their unions, or even through industrial action, now have little prospect of success through such methods. Given the difficulty of increasing the gross level of wages, they have become more concerned with containing the size of the figure in the box marked 'deductions' in the corner of their pay slip.

Reducing the election debate to a quibble over tax also has the effect of reducing the electorate to the narrow band of taxpayers who are directly affected by the changes under discussion. When the Tories appealed to 'the taxpayer' in the past, they used this term to blur the division between the capitalist elite and their middle class base of support. When Tony Blair and New Labour adjust their manifesto commitments to appeal to 'the taxpayer', they invite the 1.5m voters of Middle England to decide the outcome of the political process. Worse, they invite everybody else to look at the world from the perspective of the petty pre-occupations of a section of the middle classes.

As a result of the narrowing of the terms of politics, popular opinion carries less weight in public life than at any time since the introduction of adult suffrage. Popular disenchantment with the main political parties mirrors the narrowing of options and of debate. But what are we to put in the place of the discredited politics of the past? Before looking further at some of the consequences of this disenchantment, let us look briefly at one attempt to offer a political alternative.

The exhaustion of the mainstream political traditions of British society encourages a widespread conviction that everything has been tried and has failed. It has become fashionable to decry political parties based on class interests and 'ideological' programmes, in favour of a turn to single-issue campaigns, which can attract supporters from all sections of society for their non-hierarchical mode of organisation and orientation towards practical activity. The launch in early 1996 of the Real World Coalition, a body bringing together more than 30 voluntary and 'non-governmental organisations' concerned with environmental issues, poverty and democratic renewal (and claiming to represent 2.1m members and supporters) was justified by a 'substantial groundswell of public opinion in the UK in favour of a "new politics"'. (*The Politics of the Real World,* 1996, pviii)

But this 'new politics' appears in many ways to be worse than the old. Indeed, for all its radical rhetoric, the Real World Coalition seems very close to the real world of the old establishment and highly dependent on its patronage. Its manifesto proclaims the most modest ambition of putting 'pressure on political parties' and 'influencing the political system'. A glance at the list of coalition members reveals some major international aid organisations—like Oxfam and Save the Children—with multi-million pound budgets, royal sponsors and hundreds of paid workers. Others are closely liked to the churches— Christian Aid, Catholic Institute of International Relations, Kairos, Church Action on Poverty. Others are dependent on local government support.

Even by comparison with the old parties, the Real World Coalition is highly autocratic. The first time that the vast majority of the 2.1m members of the coalition knew about its existence was probably when it was announced in the press. The first glimpse they got of its manifesto was when (if!) they bought a copy in a bookshop. While it is true that Labour and Tory leaders may not take much notice of their party conferences, at least they acknowledge the possibility of the democratic partic- ipation of the membership in policy-making.

It appears that *The Politics of the Real World* was written by one person, discussed with a few pals, vetted by a committee of representatives of the key coalition members and then rubber-stamped by other signatories on behalf of their mass memberships. This is a procedure that makes the role of union block votes at Labour Party conference look like a model of mass participation. No doubt the 2.1m will be reassured by the author's acknowledgement of 'various extremely helpful but unnameable officials of government departments and international agencies' (*The Politics of the Real World*, pxiv).

If the old parties are class-based, the mode of operation of some of the Real World Coalition members is positively feudal. Many of the environmental and charitable organisations give special prominence to their royal or aristocratic patrons or sponsors; professional and scientific experts decide policy and ordinary volunteers do the day-to-day work. Even the campaigns against new roads (which have affiliated to the coalition through their umbrella group, Alarm UK) like to find a peer of the realm or otherwise titled dignitary to speak to the press, while the more proletarian types grapple with bailiffs in the mud.

It is not surprising that the deferential attitude of the groups in the Real World Coalition towards the political establishment is rewarded with substantial subsidies and an overwhelmingly sympathetic profile in the media. The uncritical use of Greenpeace videos in television news reports has attracted some criticism, but it is only an extreme example of a general trend (Greenpeace, as an international organisation, is not itself a member of the Real World Coalition). The conservative political programme of the Real World Coalition and its member organisations, which we consider elsewhere in this book, is of course also crucial to the way they are treated by the media. This is an alternative to mainstream politics which simply puts a new face on old politics and can ultimately only reinforce the prevailing climate of anti-politics.

THE RETREAT FROM POLITICS

Disillusionment with politics does not only affect the mainstream parties, but leads to a wider disengagement from public life. Church attendance declined from eight million in 1970 to 6.7m in 1992. Long-established mass organisations such as the National Federation of Women's Institutes, the Mothers Union and the National Union of Townswomen's Guilds have lost half their members since 1971. The Red Cross Society, the British Legion, the RSPCA, the Scouts and Guides have all lost members over the past 20 years. (See *Social Trends 24*, 1994) Indeed virtually all major public institutions, from the Farmers Union to the Green Party have experienced a decline in popular participation.

More passive and individuated kinds of public involvement, on the other hand, have been increasing. More people write to local councillors, MPs and newspapers, and complaints to the ombudsman between 1976 and 1992 have doubled in relation to health and, increased by a factor of 10 in local government matters. The workloads of bodies such as Citizens Advice Bureaux, law centres, the Equal Opportunities Commission and the Commission for Racial Equality have approximately doubled over the past decade. It would appear that these semi-official bodies have taken up the strain of dissatisfaction expressed in an individualised form, as the scope for collective protests has narrowed.

Many more people give to charity, and fundraising for charity in diverse ways, from national 'telethons' and events like 'Live Aid', 'Red Nose Day' and 'AIDS week', has become a major focus of interest and activity. The total income of charities increased from £320m in 1981 to £793m in 1993, adjusted for inflation (*Social Trends 24*). There has also been a significant increase in voluntary activity in relation to education (school governors, parent-teachers associations), health (there are now support groups, self-help groups and campaigns around every major disease or disorder—even around many rare conditions) and other areas from child welfare and protection to care of the old and mentally ill.

Perhaps the most significant manifestation of the recognition that mainstream politics is exhausted at a time when there is such a heightened awareness of the insecurity of everyday life is the tendency to become preoccupied with the self and with individual survival. A lack of consistency or direction in politics goes hand in hand with confusion and disorientation in the workplace and the home, in professional and personal relationships. From this perspective the quest for personal redemption takes priority over any attempt to engage with society.

● the workplace

The workplace has come to be regarded as a source of many new problems which both express and reinforce feelings of insecurity. In the past employees' main concern in the workplace was with wages, and the need to organise to get the employers to raise them. Today what are perceived as the problems at work are much more diverse, and the employer is more likely to be regarded as a potential source of support than as the source of the problem.

For example, issues of health and safety have acquired central importance. If workers take industrial action today they are more likely to try to justify their action on the basis of their concern for the safety of staff, consumers or service-users, than in terms of their need for higher wages. Union leaders involved in recent strikes on the railways have always emphasised their concern that the safety of the public was being put in jeopardy by new work schedules, using non-union members to drive trains, cutting back on guards, etc.

Though unions have always been concerned about the health and safety of their members, this problem has acquired much greater dimensions in recent years. In the past the main threat to safety was identified as employers or managers concerned to maximise productivity by cutting corners, curtailing safety regulations and forcing workers to take risks. Today the source of the problem is just as likely to be seen as a fellow worker engaged in bullying colleagues or causing a health risk by smoking. Other sources of danger are angry customers or, in public services, members of the public. People at work are now also considered to be highly vulnerable to harassment on grounds of race, gender or sexual orientation. There is, too, the fear that workers may be a danger to themselves (as well as to others) as a result of drinking alcohol (especially in lunch breaks) or taking drugs.

The response of employers in workplaces in both private and public sectors has been to draw up detailed codes of practice to regulate behaviour in these areas—often at the behest of the unions. Many also send employees on special courses to enhance their awareness of these problems and to train them in tactics for coping. The question of random screening tests for alcohol and drug abuse—now a widespread practice in the USA—is just coming into discussion in Britain. The preoccupation with safety leads to the more intensive regulation of day-to-day matters in the workplace, without providing any guarantee of safety. Indeed the general drift of all these initiatives is to make issues of health and safety more the responsibility of workers and less that of employers.

In the past workers used to complain that they suffered from poor pay and conditions, long hours and fear of redundancy. Now they complain of *stress,* which surveys confirm has reached epidemic proportions in Britain's workplaces. This redefinition of the problem has important consequences. When workers complained about pay and conditions and blamed them on the employers, the logical course of action was to join a union and press for action to make management concede improvements. But if the complaint is stress, then the logical response is to seek some psychological assistance or some counselling, which may well be provided by the modern ethical employer as a special service to the workforce. The stress syndrome transforms a potential trade union militant into a helpless victim.

The promotion of safety in the workplace enhances managerial authority while confirming the vulnerability and powerlessness of workers. It encourages the notion that 'someone else' will help to solve your problems—and that 'someone else' is, as often as not, your employer, whose pay and productivity policies are probably the source of most of the problems in the first place.

● education

For everybody from government ministers to unemployed youth in the UK, education appears to have become the last great hope. The merger of the departments of education and employment reflects the Tory government's conviction that education and training are the answer to the problems of the national economy and the labour market. In a similar spirit, New Labour appears to have reduced economic policy to proposals for education and training. Whether you are an unemployed school-leaver, somebody made redundant at the height of your working life or forced to take early retirement a decade or more before you can collect your (increasingly meagre) pension, the message is no longer 'get on your bike' to look for work (everybody now knows there is nowhere to go); the message of the 1990s is 'get on a course'. Instead of a 'job for life', everybody is now offered a lifetime of training and education as the only way of coping with the transformations of the labour market wrought by new technology and globalisation.

One consequence of recruiting the nation's teachers to help clean up the mess which economic crisis has made of the labour market is the degradation of education itself. In particular the distinction between a broad education for life and the narrow requirements of vocational training is being lost. The government's school curriculum supremo Ron Dearing justified his early 1996 proposals for more 'vocational A-levels' by equating intellectual and practical skills, arguing that 'our economic future lies in creating a highly educated, well-trained and adaptable workforce' (*Independent,* 28 March 1996).

But the attainment of academic excellence and the development of practical skills are not of equal value, either to the individual or to society. Competence in building a wall or perming a head of hair is not on a par with the ability to analyse a historical document, write a critique of the narrative technique in *Wuthering Heights* or consider the theoretical complexities of quantum mechanics. Training enables people to acquire practical skills in occupational areas already established by the existing division of labour in society. Education aims to develop capacities of independent thinking and initiative that can enhance the higher human potentialities of innovation and creativity that are crucial to the advance of civilisation.

In the past, it has generally been recognised that education needs a degree of autonomy from the demands of the capitalist economy if it is to fulfil its civilising role in society. Demands for the subordination of education to economic expediency have always been dismissed as crass and shortsighted. Indeed earlier Conservative government initiatives to elevate vocational training to the status of education were widely condemned. Yet, such is the spirit of desperation abroad today, the barbarians have been unleashed and scarcely a voice is now raised in defence of learning. The old polytechnics have been renamed as universities and vocational qualifications (such as NVQs) have been designated as equivalent to academic qualifications (such as GCSEs).

More and more people enter further and higher education, only to receive a lower standard of education and a degraded degree.

The extension of vocational training around NVQs has also degraded training. Whereas vocational training in the old apprenticeship system involved the acquisition of genuine skills, many NVQs are simply attempts to dignify unskilled work, like emptying bed pans and talking sympathetically to old people, or filing and being friendly to customers. It is striking that many industries in which real training is required, such as engineering, have rejected NVQs as inappropriate.

Given the promotion of education as the solution to the problems of the nation, it is not surprising that it has become a preoccupation for many parents, who have come to regard the acquisition of educational qualifications as the only guarantee of a secure future for their children. The government's emphasis on standards, testing and league tables and its encouragement of schools to 'opt out' of local authority control have intensified parental concerns about finding the right school for their child. The controversies provoked by Tony Blair's and Harriet Harman's selection of schools for their children underline how central this issue has become for parents throughout the country.

Young people seem to agree that without education the future is bleak: 'Teenagers of all abilities and social classes are coming to accept that further education and university are for them, and that without them their employment prospects are blighted.' (*Financial Times,* 17 August 1995) But is education the solution to all our problems?

Leading US economist Paul Krugman is sceptical: 'It is hard to escape the feeling that those who place their faith in education and training as the major solution to the problems of jobs and wages are engaged in wishful thinking.' (*Independent on Sunday*, 16 October 1994) Another American commentator, Simon Head, agrees:

> We constantly hear from Democratic politicians and from corporate executives like Bill Gates that "education" must be improved if it is to counter the effects of corporate downsizing....But it is an illusion to believe that...job programmes can by themselves create in significant numbers the secure, well-paid and relatively high-skilled jobs that members of the middle class have traditionally held. (*The New York Review of Books*, 29 February 1996)

Several detailed studies of job vacancies have begun to expose the notion of a 'skills shortage' as a myth (see P Meadows, *et al*, *The London Labour Market*, 1988; IFF, *Research, Vacancies and Recruitment Study*, 1988; C Marsh, 'The road to recovery?', *Work, Employment and Society*, March 1990). This notion has become a new scapegoat for the failings of an economic system which, because it must subordinate all else to the pursuit of profit, cannot sustain consistent productive investment and growth.

The current obsession with training shifts the social problems of unemployment and insecure employment into the sphere of education. After first blaming teachers for poor educational standards, the focus has now shifted on to students (of every age) who do not take their personal learning responsibilities seriously.

According to Christopher Bell, chair of the Campaign for Learning, 'the mission is to persuade people that they should care about their personal training in the same way that we are all gradually learning to care about the environment and our own health' (*Independent,* 25 April 1996). The problem is that taking individual responsibility for a system that cannot provide jobs for the most highly trained individuals can only intensify personal demoralisation.

● health

The publication of the government white paper *The Health of the Nation* in 1992 marked the promotion of health to the level of a national obsession. The white paper emphasised the links between a high fat diet, lack of exercise, smoking, alcohol and 'unsafe' sex and 'modern epidemics' of coronary heart disease, cancer, liver disease and sexually transmitted diseases, most notably AIDS. It set targets for the reduction of death rates from these conditions and exhorted everybody to take greater personal responsibility for their own health.

The message of *The Health of the Nation* has been transmitted in the most diverse ways, through the media, through the health service (in particular through the radical reorganisation of general practice around the requirements of 'health promotion') and through the schools. As we have seen in our earlier discussion of the health scares which have raged relentlessly over the past decade (Chapter Two), there is a ready response for concerns about disease and death in an already introspective and depressed society. The fads for jogging and running, for aerobics and weight training, and the apparently insatiable public appetite for features about health in women's magazines, men's magazines, in television documentaries (and medical soaps) all confirm the extent of the modern preoccupation.

One of the paradoxes of the health obsession is that it has emerged at a time when Western society enjoys the highest standard of health and the longest life expectancy in human history. Never in history have so many healthy people felt so ill. Another curious feature of the promotion—and widespread acceptance—of the gospel of 'healthy lifestyles' is that there is little evidence to suggest that they will make much difference to health or longevity.

Take, for example, the dietary approach to heart disease (see M Fitzpatrick, 'Healthy eating in a diseased society', *Living Marxism,* January 1995). The problem here is that, though diverse 'associations' and 'risk factors' have been identified, the causes of this condition remain obscure and treatment remains largely unsatisfactory. Furthermore, because it is a disease of age-ing—83 per cent of those who die of coronary disease are over 65—the scope for any intervention is limited. In response to the demonstration that a 10 per cent reduction in serum cholesterol in the population would reduce mortality from coronary heart disease by 27 per cent, it has been shown that 'expressed in terms of individual life expectancy gained, this represents only 2.5 to 5.0 months' (*British Medical Journal,* 16 April 1995, pp1038-39). Furthermore it appears that simple fat-reducing diets are ineffec-tive in producing the desired reduction in serum cholesterol, while effective diets are unpalatable and cannot be sustained.

The problem is that genetic, cultural and environmental factors, as well as chance, all appear to affect any particular individual's likelihood of developing coronary heart disease (the same applies to most forms of cancer). This means that the scope for personal initiative in improving your survival prospects through diet, exercise, etc, is relatively small.

According to the late Petr Skrabanek, a trenchant critic of the excesses of modern 'risk-factor' epidemiology, the prevailing obsession about health is 'not orchestrated by some worldwide conspiracy, but is rather the result of a positive feedback between the masses stricken by fear of death and the health promotionists seeking enrichment and power' (*The Death of Humane Medicine and the Rise of Coercive Healthism,* 1994, p38). In fact, a fear of death and anxiety about health are strongest among the middle classes, though there is a tendency for fears and prejudices of this sort to trickle down to the masses much more rapidly than wealth.

One result of a loss of faith in the future is that the meaning of life tends to shrink to become identified with its duration. In the end, all anybody has is their own lifespan and staying alive becomes an end in itself. Hence they become preoccupied with clinging on to life, with holding off death, with playing safe and avoiding risks. As Skrabanek puts it, 'a dying century and a dying culture makes war against death its main preoccupation' (*The Death of Humane Medicine and the Rise of Coercive Healthism,* p39). Paradoxically, when there appears to be nothing to live for, people are reduced to trying to prolong life itself. Yet, as Skrabanek also observes, to live in fear of death is to fear living.

Such a climate of fear is receptive to any agency that offers greater security, or any source of rules to enhance the individual's prospects of survival in a world experienced as hostile and threatening. Anxiety invites moralism and self-regulation: it thrives on the sort of guidelines governing everything from diet to sex offered by the government and the medical authorities.

In a society in which people feel they have no control over the forces that shape their lives, they can at least exert some control over their own bodies:

> Investing in the body provides people with a means of self-expression and a way of potentially feeling good and increasing the control they have over their bodies. If one feels unable to exert control over an increasingly complex society, at least one can have some effect on the size, shape and appearance of one's body. (C Shilling, *The Body and Social Theory*, 1993, p7)

In fact, control over one's own body is highly constrained by forces in wider society: there is more scope for it to be exercised negatively in the form of eating disorders and self-mutilation than in any positive sense.

Numerous commentators have noted that the evils targeted by modern health promotion are strikingly similar to the sins defined by traditional religion—from promiscuity to drunkenness and gluttony. In fact, today's health moralism is even worse: at least religion accepts the reality of suffering and offers consolation in afterlife. 'Healthism' offers only fear and guilt.

'Hope I die before I get old', sang The Who in the 1960s. In the 1990s we live in a society in which young people want only to survive to get old, while many old people struggling to survive on diminishing pensions, welfare and healthcare provision may well wish they were already dead.

UNDER SCRUTINY

All in all the degradation of the subject, the belittling of the human potential to change things for the better, is having some serious political and social consequences. It has encouraged people to withdraw into personal life, and to assume a more passive, cynical and even nihilistic attitude towards the outside world. The result is a dangerous cocktail of a loss of confidence in humanity and progress, and an abandonment of engagement with wider social issues in favour of more petty personal concerns. The sense of paralysis, that there is no alternative and nothing much can be done, is almost overwhelming.

Such paralysis would be bad enough. But there is worse to come. People are not only retreating from the social into the personal. Isolated as vulnerable individuals, who no longer feel that they can rely on the old institutions and solidarities or trust other people, they are also seeking protection. They are retreating into the personal under the scrutiny of the state.

On every issue, from what we eat to what we watch on television, there are increasing demands for more regulation and protection from one official authority or another. The degradation of the subject and the politics of paralysis are leading us down the path towards greater state supervision of more areas of life, all done in the name of protecting us from the risks and dangers that are now allegedly posed by other people, and indeed by ourselves.

The general retreat into the personal under the scrutiny of the state poses grave dangers for those of us concerned to create a better, more free, society. It is lending a fresh legitimacy to far-reaching restrictions on our liberties, as well as encouraging a cautious spirit of self-policing. Let us now turn to consider the problems raised by the rise of what we might call the new authoritarianism.

THE NEW AUTHORITARIANISM

4

Changes in the way society is governed
add up to a spectacular incursion upon our
liberties and an unprecedented extension
of official and semi-official regulation
of everyday life.

The ability to decide for yourself has been a core principle of British society—albeit one that is often denied us in the finer detail. Our long-established rights rest on that principle, that people should be free to choose for themselves how they live their lives. But what happens when we lose the habit of choosing for ourselves? In the previous chapter we saw how subjectivity, the ability of the individual to act in society, has been undermined in recent times. In this chapter we look at the way that our rights and freedoms have been subverted as a consequence.

In real terms, the assumption of individual autonomy has been overturned. Looked at dispassionately, changes in the way society is governed add up to a spectacular incursion upon our liberties and an unprecedented extension of official and semi-official regulation of everyday life.

There is today a far greater scope for surveillance and monitoring of public space. There are now more than a million cctv cameras throughout Britain: three times as many as there were three years ago. Yet the government this year announced its plans to finance a further 10 000 cctv cameras.

These sensitive surveillance systems are now common-place everywhere from public transport to public toilets. Local councils are working at high speed to install security cameras in town centres, and smaller systems are used to monitor markets, shopping centres, underground car parks and hospitals. Schools, colleges and university campuses are increasingly being equipped with the most up-to-date in surveillance technology, making them look more like open prisons than centres of learning.

Where there are no cameras, the authorities have set up and funded Neighbourhood Watch schemes, in which residents are encouraged to spy on their neighbours. The first scheme was set up in 1983; Home Office figures now estimate that there are around 30 000 of them. On top of these residents' schemes, the authorities now recruit postmen, milkmen, taxi drivers and other ordinary people—like the bloke who checks your family snaps in Boots—to keep an eye out for anything unusual in a district.

Control over residential areas has extended to an increasing number of rules governing the behaviour of each individual and family living on council estates. We have seen the introduction of the probationary tenancy, a contractual relationship between landlord and tenant pioneered by Labour-controlled local housing departments and some housing associations. Probationary tenancies rest upon the notion that the behaviour of tenants on council estates can be controlled through a period of forced obedience to the rules. The Tory government has also brought in new legislation to deal with 'anti-social behaviour', or noisy or plain nasty neighbours, and more new laws are promised by the Tories and New Labour alike.

Despite the heavy penalties it carries, the definition of what constitutes 'anti-social behaviour' is far from clear. The Department of the Environment defines it as follows: 'Such behaviour manifests itself in many different ways and at varying levels of intensity. This can include vandalism, noise, verbal and physical abuse, threats of violence, racial harassment, damage to property, trespass, nuisance from dogs, car repairs on the street, joy-riding, domestic violence, drugs and other criminal activities, such as burglary.' (Department of the Environment, Consultation Paper on Probationary Tendencies, April 1995) With so many definitions of anti-social behaviour, many of which would seem to apply to everyday life on any council estate, these look like rules which are virtually impossible to keep.

Over the past few years, the authorities have also gained far-reaching powers to monitor and intervene in the lives of anyone with children. Through the increasing preoccupation with child abuse and the increasing scope of the authorities to intervene in cases of suspected abuse, the behaviour of parents in relation to their children is becoming subject to intense regulation and control.

The Child Protection Register (also known as the 'at-risk register'), which was formalised in the 1989 Children Act, gives social workers the most far-reaching powers ever to intervene in family life. In 1990, there were 43 200 children deemed to be 'at risk', and by 1991 this number had grown to 45 300. The high number of children who are also removed from the register each year—26 200 in 1994—suggests that this intrusive system of family surveillance bears little relationship to any real incidence of child abuse (Department of Health, *Children and Young People on the Child Protection Register,* 1991, 1994). A child can be placed on the 'at-risk' register as a result of a report from a teacher, neighbour or relative. In addition to this, children themselves are increasingly encouraged to inform the authorities if they think they are being abused—a recipe for mayhem, given the normal ups and downs of family relations. The consequences of widening the powers of social workers to decide for themselves when a child is 'at-risk' and to deal with it without regard to the rights of the parents have been far-reaching and often catastrophic, most clearly in the cases of families from the Orkneys to Oxfordshire which have been broken up in the course of bogus crusades against Satanic abuse.

Outside the family, behaviour between individuals has become more closely regulated than ever before. Throughout universities, workplaces, and even schools, rules now exist to control the behaviour of individuals towards one another. These codes of conduct generally take two forms: the Equal Opportunities Policy or the Personal Harassment Policy.

The codes are as open-ended as possible, ensuring that every possible definition of offensive behaviour is covered. The National Union of Teachers' policy states that 'harassment is behaviour which has the effect of diminishing a person's position, status or self-esteem. It is imposed on an individual by another on the basis of their sex, race, sexual orientation, disability, religion, cultural or language difference, age, HIV status, or other medical conditions, physical attributes, class, race, trade union membership or political affiliation' (NUT, *Harassment: A Union Issue,* 1992).

The scope that Harassment Policies or Equal Opportunities Policies have for regulating interpersonal behaviour is enormous. The codes of conduct are always accompanied by a detailed grievance procedure, generally involving a special body of people set up to deal with cases of racial or sexual harassment. The penalties for contravening the harassment policy can range from a caution to a transfer to loss of one's job or, at a university, exclusion from the university premises.

Even the way we treat ourselves is subject to scrutiny. Often promoted on the basis of health, the 1990s has brought an explosion of rules governing personal behaviour. We noted in the previous chapter how, since the publication of the Department of Health's paper, *The Health of the Nation,* the government has sought more extensively to regulate individuals' behaviour where it is seen to constitute a 'health risk' to themselves. As the then Secretary of State for Health, William Waldegrave, said in his introduction to the paper: 'there is considerable emphasis in this document on the need for people to change their behaviour— whether on smoking, alcohol consumption, exercise, diet, avoidance of accidents and, with AIDS, sexual behaviour.' An entire industry has developed to drum these messages home and tell people how to moderate their personal behaviour.

Even the most intimate areas of life, such as sexual relationships, have become subject to intense scrutiny by the authorities. Through a discussion focused on AIDS, the government and many quangos, charities and other organisations have pushed for the regulation of individuals' sexual behaviour. The multi-million pound 'safer sex' campaign has promoted the benefits of abstinence and monogamy, awareness classes, counselling and condoms. The result has been to foster a repressive sexual code to match the Victorian model, only this time couched in terms of personal health and safety rather than religion and morality.

THE NEW AUTHORITARIANISM

Taken separately, and considered in their own terms, all of the above examples of regulation might seem relatively harmless: after all smoking is bad for you, offending people gratuitously is cruel, child abuse is damaging, noisy neighbours are a nuisance. And as the government and police are always telling us, even the widespread surveillance of public space and the removal of the right to silence need not be a problem for anyone unless they really do have something to hide.

However, when the examples given here and many more similar developments are taken together as a package and set in a wider context, a disturbing pattern emerges. The basic assumption that people should be responsible for conducting their own affairs no longer holds. This is a development which throws the 'nothing to hide' idea into question. Because what all of the above examples have in common is the assumption that we all implicitly have something to hide.

There is an ever-widening definition of what constitutes suspicious, offensive or even criminal behaviour. Disciplinarian parents who occasionally smack their kids, or doting parents collecting snaps for their photograph album—as Julia Somerville did, leading to her arrest on suspicion of sexual abuse—would not have considered themselves child abusers. But, under the 1989 Children Act and in the eyes of the NSPCC, they can now be defined as such. Colleagues who regularly made a joke about each other's dress sense or wacky beliefs may never before have considered themselves harassers, but according to their company's equal opportunities policy they could be defined as such.

It is becoming increasingly difficult for the individual to know whether he is doing wrong or not. A parent may recognise that they have a child with an overactive imagination, but if the child takes it upon himself to give Childline a call he is likely to end up on the 'at-risk' register. A tenant may have fixed his car in the street for years, but if a new tenant takes objection to this he may face eviction as a result. A male worker in an office full of women may have flirted with them for years, but if a new recruit decides that this is unacceptable behaviour the 'offender' may face the sack.

Under these new conditions we are all presumed guilty until proven innocent. By walking down the street we are all now subject to police surveillance. When applying for a tenancy, we are effectively on probation for 12 months, to make sure that we are as well behaved as we say we are. When applying for an operation, medical services will go to great lengths to find out our alcohol, cigarette and cholesterol consumption, and how much we sleep around.

The control of many aspects of our lives is being further removed from us and placed in the hands of the authorities. Our rights—to free assembly, to silence, to free speech, to determine what we do in our own homes—have become subject to more regulation. What we can or should say and do is not determined by us alone, but is increasingly influenced by somebody else in some kind of official capacity. In almost every aspect of our lives, we are being told how to behave, and often face a severe penalty if we do not comply.

ORIGIN OF THE PROBLEM

The trend outlined here has all the features of an authoritarian regime, in which the state has enormous powers to interfere in the lives of individual citizens. Restrictions on free speech and free assembly, intrusion into your personal life, the presumption of guilt; in the past these would have been seen as the tell-tale features of totalitarian regimes elsewhere in the world, the kind of thing we were told would be imposed over here if the German Nazis or Soviet communists invaded. As a result, the struggle to preserve freedom and democracy against the authoritarian state was deeply entrenched in British culture.

When George Orwell published his novel *Nineteen Eighty-Four* in 1949, it was widely interpreted as a warning about the dangers of authoritarianism. As Professor Ben Pimlott says in his introduction to the 1987 edition, the novel connected with contemporary fears: 'Totalitarianism was a stalking fear. Nazi Germany in the recent past, Russia and China in the present, framed the Western political consciousness.' Many of the extraordinary measures that symbolised the totalitarian society of *Nineteen Eighty-Four* are commonplace in 1996: video surveillance, 'sex crime', children encouraged to denounce their parents, compulsory moral lectures at work and so on.

1996, however, is not *Nineteen Eighty-Four,* and the authoritarian trends we are seeing today are very different to those that existed in the past. This is the development of a new kind of authoritarianism, one that does not impose itself from above, but is called for by society at large. In the past the parties of order in

European politics were the preserve of the gentry. But today everyone is demanding order. The value of freedom today is diminished. Instead, most people long for security, for protection against the plethora of new risks and dangers that seem to be pressing in on the anxious, vulnerable individuals who make up society today.

The freedom of the individual was a defining characteristic of the ideology of Western societies throughout the postwar era. But today it is an idea that is viewed with suspicion. Ironically the attempts to restore individual enterprise, through the defeat of the old collectivities, have done most to undermine the idea of freedom. The Conservatives thought that breaking the collective framework provided by trade unions and working class self-organisation would liberate the individual entrepreneur in us all. But the opposite happened. Once social solidarities were dismembered, individuals were left isolated and vulnerable. The confidence that collective identity and action brought was gone. Instead of being liberated as confident actors, we were left as the victims of circumstance.

With the break-up of traditional solidarity, other people become a source of fear rather than of confidence. Where once your neighbours and colleagues might have been seen as allies, today they are more likely to be seen as a potential threat or danger. It is not that people really are at war with each other. The incidences of crime, warring neighbours and harassment at work are much exaggerated. However, once the familiarity of a common endeavour and outlook is undermined things begin to look different. Other people start to look like strangers instead of friends. Innocent points of contact are seen to be fraught with danger. When you do not know your neighbours, the sound of their stereo can prey on the mind far more. If you do not know what your neighbours do for a living, it is easy to imagine that they are up to no good. If you do not socialise with your workmates then any unsolicited remark at work can sound like a put-down or carry an unpleasant innuendo. But nine times out of 10 the perception of danger is in the eye of the beholder. It is the lack of clear lines of contact that makes all contact seem risky, creating a situation where more people are open to demands for more supervision and surveillance of our affairs.

So great is the perception of risk and danger in all walks of life, that the growth of regulation and control is not itself seen to be a problem. Consequently, the only criticism that the state has faced in its growing incursion into everyday life has tended to be that it is not going far enough in protecting people.

THE DEMAND FOR ORDER

One of the key features of the new authoritarianism that dominates society today is that it is not imposed with any secrecy. On the contrary—when the authorities bring in new rules to govern our lives they go to great lengths to publicise those ways in which they intend to remove our right to autonomy and freedom.

Take, for example, security cameras. When Kings Lynn in Norfolk pioneered its town surveillance network in 1992, the local council staged a series of open seminars—The Kings Lynn Experience—to promote the capabilities of its 46-camera system.

When Brighton council made its decision to monitor the town centre in 1994, the police held public meetings with the locals in order to show off how effective their equipment was at monitoring large spaces and spotting 'suspects'.

Even the farthest-reaching measures of regulating behaviour are promoted in the most positive of ways. Apply for almost any job today and at the bottom of the advert you will be told that the company is 'an equal opportunities employer'—get the job and you will be given a glossy copy of the equal opportunities policy with its extensive rules on personal behaviour, and reassured by the personnel manager that any complaint you make against your workmates will be taken seriously.

What distinguishes this new authoritarianism most clearly from old forms of overt social control is that it is not seen as a problem. Indeed the new authoritarianism has often been invited in as a solution to society's problems. Moves to regulate more and more areas of our lives are not greeted with mass demonstrations or protests about the loss of civil liberties, but are generally welcomed or at least accepted as a fact of modern life.

According to the 1996 *British Attitudes Survey,* four out of every five people believe that covert surveillance of 'suspects' is justified, even on the basis of an anonymous tip-off (Twelfth Edition, 1995; see also R Knight, 'The new fear of crime', *Living Marxism,* January 1996). The polling organisation System 3, conducting a poll of Glaswegians' attitudes to the CityWatch cctv scheme, found that 95 per cent of Glaswegians were in favour of CityWatch, two per cent against and only seven per cent thought that it infringed their civil rights (D Cummings, *The New Glasgow: From Culture to Curfew*, Campaign Against Militarism, 1994). Whereas in the past there would have been a reaction against surveillance cameras, ID cards, censorship and the end to the right to silence, according to the *British Attitudes Survey* roughly 70 per cent of people support these measures.

Even groups which you might expect to be a little concerned about the growth of surveillance, such as the civil liberties pressure group Liberty, do not question the cameras themselves. The questions Liberty raises are simply about the regulation of the cameras. In its 1989 briefing, *Who's Watching You?: Video Surveillance in Public Places*, Liberty puts forward a series of demands for increased regulation of cctv: police access to private systems, more Home Office guidelines, and official inspection and supervision of the staff of 'a private concern'. In other words, Liberty's response to surveillance and regulation is simply to ask who is watching the people watching us, and to demand more regulation.

The main reason given for supporting authoritarian measures is fear of crime. In their 1992 paper *Closed Circuit Television in Public Places* Terry Honess and Elizabeth Charman conclude that the support for cctv among the general public was largely due to this fear. According to their survey, 92 per cent of people believe that the purpose of cctv is to 'catch criminals', 79 per cent believed that it was to 'scare off potential offenders' and 57 per cent believed it was to 'make people feel safe'. By contrast, 39 per cent thought that it was to 'check up on the general public' and 32 per cent thought it was to spy on people.

The consequences of the fear of crime are starkly illustrated by the way in which uniquely horrific crimes are now often interpreted as a general threat, and become the pretext for introducing more regulations and controls on society. In Dunblane, the slaughter of 16 schoolchildren at the hands of Thomas Hamilton spurred a discussion about the need for new laws on gun-control and more security measures in schools. The rape and murder of nine-year old Daniel Handley by Thomas Morss and Brett Tyler provoked a demand for a national register of paedophiles.

In fact the regulation of guns is comparatively strict in Britain, and no increase in controls or surveillance cameras in schools would be likely to prevent the unpredictable outburst of a lone madman. Similarly the surveillance of suspected paedophiles is already comprehensive. Since 1986 local authorities have had access to police records of criminal convictions. Since 1992 local authorities have been required to notify the Department of Health of any conduct on the part of voluntary staff that might be inappropriate for people working with children. These names are listed on a Consultancy Service Index. The comprehensive policing of sex-offenders is unlikely to have stopped Morss and Tyler. Indeed their own ill-starred relationship was begun on the sex-offenders wing of Wormwood Scrubs prison.

What are in fact extraordinary crimes are seized upon as if they were typical. The rarity of these kinds of offences does not stop them becoming the standard against which the authorities are to be measured. No amount of regulation could forestall these unique offences. But still the powers that be are called upon to prevent 'another' Dunblane massacre. These extraordinary events are seen in a particular light because of the overwhelming fear of other people. What should be seen as rare is instead seen as emblematic of the human condition. Instead of being seen as the exception, killers like Hamilton, Morss and Tyler are seen as demonstrating the evil potential we all share. The perception of danger makes more security regulations and controls seem justifiable, indeed desirable.

DO SOMETHING

Rather than simply being imposed from above by tyrannical rulers, today far-reaching measures of state intervention and control are being demanded from below. Indeed those groups and individuals at the forefront of demanding more authoritarian legislation are often those seen as most critical of the government and other state authorities. Calling for more regulation has become a focus for critics of officialdom.

For example, at the forefront of the demands for more policing of family life have been feminists like Beatrix Campbell and Anna Coote, who have called upon the government, courts and police to act to combat what they claim is a boom in child abuse and domestic violence. On slender evidence Campbell campaigned for action in Cleveland against a presumed abuse ring. Despite the collapse of the investigations in Cleveland, the Orkneys, Saundersfoot and Oxfordshire, the demand for more investigation of family life continues unabated.

The codes of conduct governing what we say and do in workplaces and colleges, such as equal opportunities and anti-harassment polices, were also demanded by the radically minded, especially women's officers within trade or student unions. A decade ago, the National Council for Civil Liberties (now renamed Liberty) was campaigning for the development of personal harassment policies, to enable employers to protect employees from sexual or racial harassment (P Stamp and S Roberts, *Changing the Workplace: Positive Action for Women,* 1986). A decade later, such codes of conduct and policies exist in every major workplace and educational institution. They have resulted in wide-ranging infringements on our right to conduct our own affairs, and allowed employers to enforce much greater controls on the way we behave. Yet the desire for regulation is such that Liberty, a campaign whose avowed aim is to promote and protect civil liberties, is proud of its record in promoting these policies.

The effect of authoritarian measures being called for by the most radical sections of society is marked. The demand for regulation is seen as a criticism of the authorities. Police officers, social workers, employers and law courts stand accused of not doing enough to protect people, while their response is often to insist that there are limits to what they can do.

FREEDOM SPURNED

The process in which radicals demand more restraints and the authorities appear to hold back has a perverse effect. It turns the reality of authoritarianism on its head. The reality is that laws, rules and regulations can only be brought in and executed by those in authority, at the expense of individuals' autonomy and freedom. However, when those at the forefront of demanding more regulation are precisely those organisations seen as campaigning for rights, the picture that emerges is rather different. Rather than the new authoritarianism being seen as the erosion of liberties at the hands of the authorities, it appears that the people with the power to protect us are refusing to do enough.

How has this inversion of reality come about? We have already examined how the climate of fear which prevails today predisposes many people to panic and demand protection. When society is so fraught with fear and uncertainty, anything from a one-off massacre of schoolchildren to unproven suspicions about British beef can fuel a scare about our own safety, or that of our children. When the dominant mood is one of fear and people feel constantly at risk and under threat, demands for protection and prevention quickly follow.

But there is something else at work here too. Even if the demands for protection were all based on real threats rather than inflated panics, this would not fully account for the apparent willingness of people to invite more regulation and give up their autonomy today. In the past it was recognised that calling for more protection from the state carried with it a penalty—the loss of individual freedom. Although that price was sometimes seen as one worth paying, the debate reflected the recognised contradiction between seeking freedom from state control and demanding protection by the state.

Today, this contradiction no longer appears to exist—or at least, few seem to recognise its existence. A discussion about the need for protection can take place with little or no reflection on the necessary infringements on our rights that this will entail. Moreover, the call for more regulation and intrusion by the authorities, of a kind which will inevitably infringe on individual autonomy, is now often put forward by those who in the past were renowned for defending civil liberties.

This could be explained if individuals and groups had simply given up on the fight for rights, and rights were seen as unimportant. However, this is not the case. A paradox of the current period is that, at a time when our rights are being eroded on all sides, rights are publicly acknowledged as more important than ever. Scarcely a day seems to go by without another right being declared for some minority group in society, or another charter issued outlining the rights of consumers. So what's going on?

A TYRANNY OF RIGHTS

There has been an apparent explosion of rights in our society over recent years. Much recent legislation and policy enshrines rights that would not have been recognised as existing in the past. The Conservative government's Citizen's Charters set out a series of rights for everybody from people buying stamps in a post office to people travelling to work on a train. Groups which never had rights before now have rights. Under the UN Convention on the Rights of the Child and the 1989 Children Act, children have rights. Under the 1986 Disabled Person's Act, disabled people have a number of rights. Even non-humans have rights. We are told of the rights of the environment, animal rights and the rights of future generations.

The proliferation of new rights over recent years is widely seen as a good thing, a sign of a freer society. And new legal rights are being demanded all the time. The campaign to have a bill of rights incorporated into British constitutional law, while unsuccessful so far, has a lot of support especially among the middle classes. Yet, despite the apparent extension of rights and the growing popularity of the language of rights, in practice real liberty is being undermined across society through the extension of multi-faceted forms of surveillance and regulation by state and para-state bodies (see J Heartfield, 'A tyranny of rights', *Living Marxism,* September 1995).

The extension of more and more rights coincides with the systematic erosion of established civil liberties and individual autonomy. On paper, people today are well supplied with rights, but in practice we have lost a lot of the real freedom to conduct our own affairs outside the reach of official surveillance and regulation.

The secret of the new authoritarianism is that an unprecedented increase of state intervention into and control over our lives has been *rendered invisible* by the endless extension of new rights. We have many new rights, which help to create the impression of a free and just society; but the meaning of rights has been degraded in such a way as to lead to the real erosion of freedom by the state.

The contemporary language of rights is a long way from the original meaning of the word. Rights have always been about winning and defending our freedom from control by the state. The right to free speech, the right to free assembly, the right to vote, the right to live as free and equal members of society; all of these great freedoms of modernity are defined by freedom from authoritarian diktat from above. Today, by contrast, every new extension of 'rights' is an extension of the authority of the state. The language of rights is today the terminology in which real freedom is being taken away. Until now the concept of right rested on the idea of a sovereign individual, making his own decisions. Today the extension of rights is about the authorities providing 'protection' and acting to infringe our autonomy.

Let us look at a couple of examples of how the concept of rights has been redefined in this way.

THE RIGHTS OF THE STATE

The way in which freedom is being undermined by the extension of rights is exemplified in many of the social policies proposed by Tony Blair's New Labour. Take, for example, the Labour Party's housing consultation paper, 'A Quiet Life'. By imposing a range of rules dictating how tenants should behave in their homes, the proposals outlined in the paper remove tenants' independence and privacy. Under the probationary tenancy scheme, tenants effectively have no rights for the first year of occupancy. Yet 'A Quiet Life' makes no mention of the removal of these basic liberties. Instead, it justifies the proposals on the basis of giving every tenant a new right: the right to a quiet life: 'Every citizen, every family, has the right to a quiet life.' In this way, the erosion of tenants' freedom is justified in terms of protecting the rights of other tenants to enjoy 'a quiet life'—whether they want it or not.

Or take the concept of children's rights, one of the clearest examples of the way in which the apparent extension of rights results in intervention by the state into families' private affairs. The UN Convention on the Rights of the Child (1989) and the 1989 Children Act establish the principle not only that children have rights, but that these rights are paramount—in other words, that they take precedence over the rights of the parents (see J Heartfield, 'Children's rights? wrong!', *Living Marxism*, October 1993). What this means is that intervention into family life by the authorities can take place in the name of the rights of the child, without regard to the rights of the parent.

This point is stated baldly in the NSPCC's summary of the principles of recent legislation: 'Children are individuals whose rights, needs and welfare are paramount. Children's needs are different to those of an adult. Intervention may be needed to fulfil those needs.' (*Words into Deeds: NSPCC Child Protection Agenda*, 1995, p4) Under these laws, any intervention which conflicts with the rights of parents can be justified on the basis that children have 'different needs' to adults, and it is the children's needs which must take priority.

In reality, the concept of children's rights is a nonsense. Because the original concept of rights meant freedom from the state, the bearers of those rights have to be capable of exercising them themselves. The reason why the right to vote is only applicable to people over the age of 18 is that children are not considered capable of making independent decisions. The fact that children have yet to learn about life through the process of education, maturation and living independently means that they cannot make rational decisions based on their own beliefs and ideas, but need to be told what to do by an adult. But today's 'rights' are not meant to be exercised by free individuals, which is why it is possible to grant such rights to minors. The state can then step in, to exercise those rights on the children's behalf— usually at the expense of the parents' rights to run their own lives.

The NSPCC's document tells us first of all that 'children are individuals'. However, because they are dependent on their parents, they are not individuals capable of fulfilling their own needs: so 'intervention may be needed' to make sure their needs are catered for. Despite the fact that they are not capable of exercising their 'rights' without intervention by the authorities, 'children have the right to be protected from abuse, neglect and exploitation' (*Words into Deeds,* p4). Working on the misanthropic assumption that abuse takes place within the family, the only body capable of exercising the child's rights for them is the state.

The prominence of so-called children's rights in today's discussions shows the extent to which real rights have been defined out of existence. The basis of the argument for rights was always the notion that the individual should have a certain amount of freedom from those in authority. Individuals were perceived as capable of making decisions, of freedom of thought and expression. The bearer of these rights was always the sovereign individual, with equal rights to everyone else.

Yet the debate about children's rights, and many of the other new 'rights' bestowed today, shows how a fundamental redefinition of rights has taken place. Rights have come to mean not freedom from the state, but protection against other people—

a child's protection against abusive parents, a quiet neighbour's protection against a noisy neighbour, a woman's protection against a potential harasser. Every right that means protection carries with it an erosion of someone else's rights. So a child's right to protection becomes an erosion of parents' right to raise a family, one neighbour's right to a quiet life becomes an erosion of another neighbour's ability to do as he pleases in his own home, and, under the broad definitions of today's codes of conduct, a woman's right not to be harassed can become the means to undermine her colleagues' right to organise their working lives.

The rights on offer today are not rights that can be borne by a sovereign individual, free from state interference. Rather, they are the rights of the victim: the victim of abuse, discrimination, a faulty product, a noisy neighbour or a colleague's sexist joke. A victim cannot exercise his rights without help from somebody with more clout—the state and its agencies. So a child who is abused will turn to the authorities to exercise his rights. A consumer who has been ripped off will turn to a lawyer to help him out. A woman who is being harassed will turn to the equal opportunities committee at her workplace in an attempt to punish her colleague. In order to have their rights exercised, victims bestow on the authorities extra power to act on their behalf.

At the end of this process, the right to protection takes precedence over real freedom and autonomy. Rights are no longer held by the individual against the state. Rights are held by the state, for use against the individual. That is the tyranny of rights that we are living under in our rights-rich, but freedom-poor, society today.

HARASSMENT AND CENSORSHIP

The problem of the new authoritarianism is a profound one in the communities, colleges and workplaces of Britain. Perhaps the intelligentsia could be expected to counter this climate of fear and repression? Hardly: authoritarian trends are even more pronounced among academics and writers than in wider society. The intelligentsia is indeed leading the way, but it is leading the way to intolerance and censorship, not freedom and liberty.

The National Union of Students (NUS) is the focal point of a new climate of intolerance in Britain's colleges and universities (see J Bristow 'Free speech supplement', *Living Marxism,* October 1995). In recent years the NUS has spearheaded campaigns to ban groups designated 'extremists', most prominently the far-right British National Party and the radical Islamic group Hizb ut-Tahrir. Leaving aside the fact that neither of these reactionary organisations had any substantial presence in British universities, the basis on which the bans were made was perverse. The bans are remarkable, not because of what they say about fascists or Islamicists, but because of what they say about NUS' view of the students it is supposed to represent. In the view of NUS, it seems, students in further and higher education could not be trusted to make up their own minds about the arguments of the BNP or Hizb ut-Tahrir, but had to be protected from exposure to such views 'for their own good'. NUS sees its own members—almost all of whom are young adults—as children in need of parental guidance over what they should or should not see and hear.

Such censorship in the colleges is now justified on the grounds that extreme views are not just objectionable, but constitute harassment that is as real as physical violence. According to NUS, the mere presence on campus of racists or Islamicists constitutes a threat to ordinary students. This takes the argument about harassment to a new low. Now even the expression of strong ideas can be considered as tantamount to an act of violence. Under the anti-harassment policies that NUS has campaigned for, and that have been taken up by most colleges, any accusation of intimidatory language can lead to bans on students and lecturers alike.

At Edinburgh University the Student Representative Council launched a campaign to stop the psychology lecturer Chris Brand teaching students (see H Guldberg 'Why ban racist Brand?', *Living Marxism,* June 1996). Brand is a self-confessed 'scientific racist' who thinks that on average blacks are genetically less intelligent than whites. According to NUS president Jim Murphy, the proposed ban was not intended to frustrate students from forming their own opinions of Brand's work, but to prevent him from intimidating 'vulnerable' students such as women and blacks. Again the core of this argument is the low opinion in which those who claim to represent students hold students themselves. It seems that students, especially female and black students, are held to be wilting wall-flowers incapable of arguing against a lecturer like Chris Brand or telling him where to get off.

Worse still, the anti-harassment campaigns are helping to create a climate of intolerance on campus. Any forthright opinion can now be considered to be harassment on no other basis than that somebody feels that they are being 'intimidated' by it.

This is a recipe for disaster. If any opinion can be banned simply because somebody finds it objectionable, and hence 'intimidatory', then there can be no defence for freedom of speech—even in the universities that are supposed to be the guarantors of intellectual freedom.

TORIES LOSE THE PLOT

The degradation of rights is the end result of a process in which freedom has become a dirty word. From left to right, all sides of the political spectrum are pursuing authoritarian social policies as the demand for order and safety has become a central concern of the day. However, the Tory right, the traditional party of law and order, has found that its old-fashioned policies of repression are out of step with the times. New Labour, on the other hand, has found it far easier to adopt and develop new authoritarian policies couched in the modern language of rights. The result has been the creation of a unique situation in which those seen as being on the left of British politics often set the law-and-order agenda around issues like noisy neighbours or paedophile registers, while those on the right have to run to catch up. The way that New Labour has become the primary sponsor of the new authoritarianism, has helped to spread further confusion about what is really going on.

Let us look a little more closely at the convergence of left and right around an authoritarian social agenda in the nineties.

The British right has always professed its affinity with the principle of liberty as against the collectivist tendencies of traditional state socialism. An example of the libertarian language of the old right is the following extract from a speech made by Thatcherite cabinet minister Norman Tebbit back in 1966:

> My beliefs, what I hold to be the principles of Conservatism, are simple. First of all that people come before the state. That a man's first loyalty is to his own principles and to his family. That Conservatives should stand for the individual, for freedom, responsibility, opportunity and free choice. Socialism seems to me to rate the state above the people, to stand for restriction, state dependency, direction and allocation and drab uniformity. (N Tebbit, *Upwardly Mobile*, 1989, p91)

The championing of individual liberties such as the Englishman's home being his castle was central to the appeal of Conservatism. Of course, the right's rhetorical belief in liberty was always limited in practice. The track record of Conservative governments is one of successive restrictions on the freedom of immigrants to enter the country, on the Irish to determine their own affairs free from military occupation, and on the rights of minorities like lesbians and gays to equal treatment in society. The brutal treatment of dissenters, such as during the miners' strike of 1984 and the poll tax riots in the late 1980s, showed that when push came to shove, the right was more concerned with controlling society than with the freedom of its citizens. But such acts of repression were largely restricted to unassimilated groups on the margins. The Tories could reassure the mainstream that they stood for liberty, while relying on the discipline of the market economy to hold society together.

Today, what preoccupies the right above all is that social cohesion seems to be failing. Once it seemed clear that people left to their own devices would spontaneously adopt the morals and values of a free market society. There was little need for official regulation to hold things together. Today, however, there is little faith in the capacity of these moral values to reproduce themselves in the lives and outlooks of ordinary people.

This is clearest in the recurrent discussion about family breakdown. In a speech to the House of Lords, Conservative peer Baroness Young summed up the fear that the breakdown of the traditional family would result in a society spinning out of control. After reeling off a catalogue of figures relating the increase in the number of divorces, cohabitees, single-parent families and children born out of wedlock, she concluded that:

> it is not an exaggeration to say that there is a real danger of a breakdown in the fabric of society. If we were to be here in five years' time what would be the statistics on this? There would be more divorces, more children born out of wedlock and more single-parent families. We are going down, at a very fast pace, an extremely slippery slope and no one knows what it will bring. (*House of Lords Official Report,* Vol552 No45 Col636, May 1994)

These dire warnings about the impending breakdown of society indicate the Tories' worst fears. Their fear is that traditional capitalist values—such as support for the nuclear family, the flag and the free market—are no longer being spontaneously reproduced in our changing society. That is why, from the late eighties and into the nineties, the Tory government and the state officials allied to it have tried to reimpose their values on society. But they have found that attempts to appeal to the old morality simply do not work. John Major's famous 'Back to basics' campaign, launched in a speech to the Tory Party conference in October 1993, in which he appealed for a return to 'good old-fashioned family values', was soon sunk in a storm of public indignation about Tory hypocrisy. The repeated failure of Tory ministers' attempt to launch a popular crusade against single mothers seemed to confirm the irrelevance of traditional Tory moralising. The government's law-and-order campaign, once its biggest asset, has also faltered badly, with Home Secretary Michael Howard reduced to a figure of public scorn and contempt.

The right is concerned to put social control before individual liberty today, but its old authoritarian morals and policing policies are no longer up to the job. Indeed, attempts to impose some old-fashioned order often backfire. So it was that in 1995, when Metropolitan Police Commissioner Sir Paul Condon sought to justify a forthcoming stop-and-search crackdown by announcing that most muggers in London were black (a tactic which had worked well for several of his predecessors), he found himself unexpectedly caught up in a public furore about racism.

The basis of the Conservatives' campaign was always rather narrowly defined. Drawing on their instincts, Tories were concerned primarily with the question of crimes against property. As long as 'law and order' meant mainly a response to theft and vandalism it was a direct appeal from Tory HQ in Smith Square to middle class property owners.

But increasingly the issue of 'law and order' has been broadened. Today's criminologists have pushed the ever-plastic definition of crime much more in the direction of crimes against the person. In fact the crime issue today is much more of a cipher for social breakdown generally than a specific appeal to the propertied classes. As the law-and-order question has been embraced by wider sections of society its character has changed. The Conservative Party, with its elitist concerns has little to say to voters for whom the fear of crime is predominantly a fear of social breakdown.

The Tories sense that some new measures of control are needed, but they are often too wedded to the past to carry them off. New Labour, on the other hand, has already cut its links with most of its past traditions and dumped its old ideological baggage. It is better placed to develop a new doctrine of social control that is relevant to the 1990s. So the baton has passed to New Labour, and the politicians and writers of the 'left' have become the primary authors of the new authoritarianism.

THE AUTHORITARIAN LEFT

The left was traditionally concerned to uphold those rights and liberties which would give the masses more influence on the political realm. So, for example, the right to join trade unions, the right to protest and to strike, and to a lesser extent equal rights for women, black people and homosexuals, all became issues for the left. As the constituency of the right was the establishment and its conservative middle class allies, the core constituency of the left was the organised labour movement and its more radical middle class allies. While the right's prime concern was with the continuation of the present system, the left's concern was with its reform.

But even more than the right, the left has suffered from the collapse of the old political framework. The stagnation of the British economy has frustrated the prospects of welfare reform over the past 20 years. And the political defeat of the old labour movement has fragmented the left's traditional constituency. Unable to offer the prospect of real change, the left lost support and paid a heavy price at the polls.

With its working class constituency politically deactivated, the Labour Party has become much more responsive to the concerns of the middle classes. Labour's middle class supporters were always concerned to defend their interests against the insecurity of the free market. Now that middle class concerns dominate New Labour's agenda, symbolised by Tony Blair's crusade to win the support of 'Middle England', the search for security and safety has become a central theme of what passes for 'left-wing' politics.

The hallmark of left-wing politics today is that it constantly draws attention to the problems in society, reflecting the disenchantment of the middle classes with the world. However, in drawing attention to these problems, the left poses no social alternative. Since New Labour has embraced the doctrine of Tina, it can present no alternative to the capitalist market as the organising principle of society. If it is not seen as possible to change the way in which society as a whole is organised, then the horizons of reform must be lowered to the level of the individual citizen. As a result, what would once have been viewed as social problems become redefined as problems of individual behaviour, and the central solution to these problems becomes the closer regulation of individual behaviour.

This pattern runs throughout Labour Party politics now. 'The right to a quiet life' recognises a social problem—that people on council estates have to put up with crowded, noisy accommodation and live in close proximity with people they do not necessarily get on with. Rather than offering a social solution, however, such as investment in improving the conditions and environment on council estates, New Labour prioritises a solution which aims at dealing only with the consequences of overcrowding: forcing individuals to behave in a certain way, and penalising those that will not.

Tony Blair's promise to be 'tough on crime and tough on the causes of crime' might sound as if it has something in common with the traditional left-wing view that crime was caused by social factors such as poverty and unemployment. However, the old left-wing solution rested on an attempt to improve the quality of people's lives so they were not tempted to commit a crime—a view with which authoritarian New Labour has little sympathy. As Peter Mandelson and Roger Liddle's mission statement for New Labour says: 'Too often in the past the left-of-centre's natural sympathy for those affected by social ills has sounded like being soft on the criminal.' (*The Blair Revolution*, p133)

When talking about the 'causes of crime', New Labour primarily has in mind not social causes that can be addressed through reform, but the bad upbringing of young people by incompetent parents:

> The problem of crime is to a large extent the problem of disaffected teenagers...who are out of control of their parents and alienated if not truant from school, or perhaps excluded as a result of disciplinary action. (*The Blair Revolution*, p134)

Their solution to the 'causes of crime' is therefore a range of authoritarian policies aimed at keeping children in school—such as fining the parents of children who truant; the appointment of an 'adult mentor' to keep a constant watch on the 'problem teenager' and to 'act as a surrogate parent for the one who either doesn't exist or isn't up to the job'; and ultimately, in shadow home secretary Jack Straw's plan for a curfew, to send social workers and policemen to round up the mythical hordes of children who are supposedly terrorising the streets of Britain.

In fact 'getting tough on crime' is now much more than a plank in Labour's platform. It is the defining ethos of New Labour's social policy. Every aspect of Labour's policy has been redefined in terms of 'fighting crime'. Whether it is education or housing, Labour's avowed motivation is to 'fight crime'. Already in Labour-controlled local authorities, any new spending is justified in terms of crime prevention. Under a Labour government we can expect the subordination of social policy to fighting crime to be even more severe. Stripped of its scare tactics about rising crime, what Labour is saying is that all social policy is about social control. The gradual redefinition of everyday behaviour in legal terms means that more and more aspects of our lives are brought under state scrutiny. The prospect of a Labour government preoccupied with social order does not bode well for our liberties (see A Calcutt, 'New Labour: the law 'n' order party', *Living Marxism,* December 1995).

The compulsion to impose order by regulating the behaviour of individuals is the point at which the politics of left and right come together today. For the right, the decline of traditional morality and what is perceived as a collapse of traditional institutions through which individuals' behaviour was kept in check has led to an almost panicked desire to clamp down in as many ways as possible, before society disappears down Baroness Young's 'slippery slope'. For the left, the compulsion to clamp down arises from its orientation towards the narrow concerns of the middle classes and its lack of an alternative social solution. Both left and right have converged around the middle class fear of disorder and the Thatcherite notion that there is no alternative to the way in which capitalist society is organised. The consensus is that only individual behaviour can and should be changed, and the only solution coming from this consensus is for increased regulation of our lives by the authorities.

For all the talk of rights today, across the political spectrum, nobody is prepared to stand up for our real right to liberty and autonomy. From the far right to the radical left, political parties and pressure groups are for bringing in more measures to control the behaviour of individuals. Worse, when the authorities are not implementing measures to control our behaviour, the public and the media are demanding more of these measures: to control our consumption of beef, our safety on the street or the behaviour of our colleagues at work.

The consequence of calling for the state to deal with our problems is that people who have an interest in changing society become less and less able to do so. They become mere spectators, calling from the sidelines for more regulation and surveillance, while our freedom to tackle problems is subordinated to the state's attempts to keep control. In April 1996, the shadow home secretary Jack Straw called for the introduction of random stop-and-search powers for the police. As things stand, the number of people stopped and searched rose by 20 per cent in 1995 to a total of 690 300 people—a figure that has risen six-fold since such powers were introduced under the 1984 Police and Criminal Evidence Act (*Guardian,* 29 June 1996). But Straw is not interested in civil liberties, arguing that 'there are no civil liberties which can be exercised from the grave'. Setting aside the rarity of homicide in the UK (just 870 people were murdered in 1992, for example), Straw's argument is depressingly authoritarian: surviving safely under the state's protection becomes all that we have the right to expect; and as long as we are alive, our rights and freedoms are considered to be of no importance. That is the central problem facing those who remain committed to real freedom today.

WHATEVER HAPPENED TO DEMOCRACY?

Parliament is increasingly side-stepped
by the judiciary, the quangos and Brussels.
And these infringements of democracy
are championed by the radical critics
of Westminister.

Everybody you talk to knows that there is something wrong with the British political system. But the real problems start when it comes to discussing how to change it. Because one thing which all of the proposed reforms seem to share is the desire to remove power further away from the real roots of democracy—*demos,* the people—and invest it instead in the hands of unelected, unaccountable authorities, be they judges, quangos, non-governmental organisations or ombudsmen. The discussion of democracy in Britain today is an example of a situation where many of those critical of the status quo have ended up proposing alternatives which would make matters even worse.

DEMOCRACY ON THE DEFENSIVE

Once seen as the Mother of Parliaments, today Westminster is widely viewed as a crotchety old fogey. Even a member of parliament like Calum MacDonald, Labour MP for the Western Isles, will now criticise the House of Commons as outmoded, trapped in an adversarial style of debate that is neither effective as government, nor convincing for an electorate:

> The adversarial culture is hostile to good government. The public is offended by the tribal rituals of parliament. They might enjoy it as daytime soap, but they do not respect it as policy-making. (Speech to the *Guardian's* What's Left conference, June 1994)

In May 1996 Ann Taylor, shadow leader of the House of Commons proposed a reform of parliamentary question time, saying that 'there is no doubt that the "yah boo" confrontational style of questions does not find favour with the electorate' (Charter 88 seminar, 'New politics, new parliament'). A month earlier the Real World Coalition had launched its manifesto as a response to a situation in which it saw mainstream politics becoming divorced from the 'real world':

> Many people today feel that something has gone wrong with British society and British politics....Yet the political system barely seems to register what is happening. It is hardly surprising that public disillusionment with politicians and parliament has never been higher. (*The Politics of the Real World*, pi).

It is striking that such anxieties should be expressed only seven years after the collapse of the Stalinist states of Eastern Europe led to a celebration of the Westminster model of democratic government. The then prime minister Margaret Thatcher boasted that the West had won the Cold War, and that the countries of the East were looking to Britain as a model of good government. In Africa and the Third World, meanwhile, British officials were advising countries like South Africa and Kenya on the conduct of free elections and the formation of democratic governments. Now, it seems, nobody is very impressed with Britain's democratic tradition.

You might have thought that the coming general election in Britain would at least generate a renewed burst of enthusiasm for democracy. After 17 years in power, every opinion poll and by-election suggests that it is more than likely that the Conservative

Party will fail to win over a critical and informed electorate. As the most unpopular administration in memory prepares to face the final judgement of the people, the Conservatives' critics might be expected to celebrate the virtues of the democratic system.

But despite this, the intelligentsia are today more critical of the political process than ever before. In books, articles, speeches and pamphlets, the educated classes denounce the bankruptcy of the British political system. Geoff Mulgan, director of the think-tank Demos, believes that the legacy of the Westminster model of government 'has turned from an enormous source of pride into an impediment' (G Radice (ed), *What Needs to Change,* p220). Nor, indeed are criticisms restricted to the chattering classes. Popular revulsion at the behaviour of politicians is at an all-time high.

Attitudes to politicians are particularly distant among the young. A recent survey of 15 to 35-year olds found that 47 per cent were 'not very' or 'not at all' interested in politics. Under-25s were more likely to attribute their lack of interest to not knowing enough, while over 25-year olds were more likely to say that they did not believe a word politicians say (quoted in *M-Power,* Young Voter Registration Campaign, Local Coordinator Pack, 1995). According to Ann Taylor, 'every Labour canvasser has tales to tell of the excluded class, of people who are utterly unaware of the value of casting a simple vote, or more depressing still, those who dismiss the act as valueless'.

Labour's canvassers might think it depressing that young people show little interest in voting, but they should not find it surprising. In the age of Tina, when little separates the programmes of the major parties, the electoral contest is less inspiring than at any time in living memory. As we have already noted, there is no real ideological battle between competing visions of society. With so little to choose between a Blair, a Major or an Ashdown, and so little on offer from any of them, nobody should be shocked to discover a lack of genuine enthusiasm for taking sides in the election.

The success of New Labour in reconstructing itself as a party of government that can be trusted by Middle England and the City of London has come at a high price. Taking the lesson that 'old Labour' was unelectable, the Blair team has set about jettisoning every policy, organisational structure and association that identified it with the past. The Labour leadership has turned its back on the policies that traditionally made the party appear distinctive, ditching every totem from nationalisation and welfarism to nuclear disarmament and support for the unions. New Labour has embraced the message that 'There is no alternative' with the vigour of a convert.

Labour's transformation, coupled with the exhaustion of the Tories' political programme, has had a marked effect on the debate between the parties in parliament and beyond. It has become a hollow affair in which personality clashes substitute for real political differences. Set-piece confrontations between Blair and Major and their lieutenants are exercises in petty point-scoring. The clash between the Home Secretary Michael Howard and his Labour opposite number Jack Straw exemplifies this vituperative non-debate. Howard and Straw concur on the desirability of draconian changes in sentencing and punishment policies. Yet each attempts to cast the other in the role of the villain's friend. Without any genuine clash of conflicting political views, the debate descends into an exchange of personal insults (see F Füredi, 'What's left and who's right now?', *Living Marxism,* April 1995).

The fact that much parliamentary debate today is a display of personal animosity without principled difference makes many people open to arguments against the 'adversarial' culture of parliament. The ritual clashes in the House of Commons are often compared unfavourably to the more business-like and consensual deliberations of the commons select committees. It is argued that these committees, made up of MPs from all parties working together, are more successful because they are free from party ideology, concentrating instead on getting results. The Labour Party's proposals for reforming parliament include handing more power to the select committees.

But the real weakness of parliament is not that it is too 'adversarial', too overburdened with ideological conflicts. Rather, the loud clash of real differences of principle is precisely what is lacking in the debates about Britain's future. The shift from making policy in the chamber of the commons to making it in the select committees can only accelerate the move towards a depoliticised system of government; one in which the technical expertise of an administrative bureaucrat counts for more than the principles of a political leader.

That might sound fair enough to many people who are disenchanted with the unprincipled gang of politicians on offer today. The trouble is, however, that this process is having a detrimental effect on the weight given to popular opinion. Today voters are expected to choose their politicians, but not their politics. The major parties become more and more like the big banks; grey institutions, distinguished from one another only by their logos and the celebrities they use in their adverts, and run by faceless administrators who burrow away in committee rooms pursuing almost identical strategies for cost-control and business efficiency. An electorate asked to choose between such non-political parties is being denied any real say in deciding how society should be run. More than ever before, the election becomes a fraudulent sham in which, whoever wins, the government gets in.

CONTRACTING DEMOCRACY

As the public political sphere shrinks, the very way in which Britain is governed is changing. The authority of government is premised upon popular participation in its decision-making, through political representation. But parliament, like other established institutions of the state, from the monarchy to the Church of England, no longer enjoys the old legitimacy in the public eye. As traditional institutions falter and fail, new forms of state power rush to fill the vacuum.

The exhaustion of the political system reaches the point of sclerosis when different institutions intrude to supplement the faltering authority of the elected government. As the palace of Westminster is no longer credited with the respect it once enjoyed, other state institutions bear the weight of social control and regulation. Three distinctive sources of authority can be seen to have been pushed to the fore as parliament fails.

Firstly 'quangos', quasi-autonomous non-governmental organisations, can be seen to have supplemented many functions of government both locally and, especially in the spheres of health and welfare, nationally. Secondly, judges have come to play an increased role in checking the government of the day: see the courts' successive rulings against the Home Secretary on matters ranging from sentencing to asylum, or the way that the Nolan committee on public standards and the Scott inquiry into the arms-to-Iraq affair have subordinated the conduct of ministers and MPs to judges' rules. Finally, the European Union and the European court have increasingly become a focus for political reform, as people have become frustrated with the intractability of the Westminster political process.

Each of these incursions by unelected bodies in the governance of Britain challenges the authority of an elected parliament. But because the public authority of parliament is at such a low ebb, little opposition has been expressed to these autocratic supplements to state power. Rather, the intervention of each of these different institutions finds a measure of support among those who are frustrated with the failure of government action. Many now look to the courts or to Europe as a way of resolving the crisis of the British system and achieving fairer government. In fact, the increasing role of these unaccountable institutions in running society only confirms the decay of popular democracy in the age of the new authoritarianism.

THE QUANGOCRACY

Quangos have been one of the few growth industries of recent years. They have often been criticised for providing overpaid and easy jobs for the boys, appointed by government ministers. Revelations of how much top quangoites get for doing how little—for example, the chairman of the Port of London Authority is reportedly paid £50 000 for attending 12 meetings a year—cause periodic outrage in the press (see, for example, *Guardian*, 11 April 1996). The Labour Party argues that quangos have blossomed under the supposedly anti-bureaucracy Conservatives, and that the personnel of these seems heavily drawn from the families and friends of the Conservative Party. Lord Nolan has indicated that he will recommend the end of the big-money posts, on the principle that public service should be a privilege in its own right, not a money-spinner for people who are already well paid.

But the trouble with quangos goes much deeper than questions of who sits on them and how much they are paid. Even if they were staffed entirely by impoverished saints, the rise of the quango is an aspect of the transfer of state functions to unelected and unaccountable bodies. As such, it can only undermine the extent of democratic government. The more authority the quangos have, the less elected bodies enjoy, and the less democratic the system of government becomes.

Despite the Tories' rhetorical commitments to abolishing bureaucracy and cutting 'red tape', the policies pursued by the Conservative government over the past 17 years have been bound to lead to the extension of the quangocracy. The government's strategy has been to undermine the role of traditional centres of local administration, many of which were elected and Labour-influenced. Metropolitan, regional and local councils, along with local health and education authorities, have all had their powers either removed or reduced. The result was to create a power vacuum. That vacuum has been filled by ever-greater numbers of quangos, whether these are NHS trusts, the governing bodies of opted-out schools or the many new urban development corporations.

In 1994 'Democratic Audit' and Charter 88 published an investigation of the extent of quangos (*EGO Trip*). They found no less than 5521 quangos, responsible for spending £48.1 billion a year. Looking at the question of finance alone, that means unelected quangos already have control over a sixth of total government expenditure.

There are now almost three times as many people serving on quangos as there are elected representatives in local and county councils and the House of Commons: 70 000 as against 25 600. The substantial change brought about by the Tory assault on local government has not been to slash public expenditure, but to remove it from democratic control or even public scrutiny. Simon Jenkins gives the example of London, where the change has been starkest with the abolition of the Greater London Council:

> in the 1890s Londoners elected 12 000 citizens to serve on councils, boards and committees....Today roughly 12 000 Londoners still sit on boards administering local services in the capital. The difference is that just 1914 are elected. The vast majority are appointed by

central government. (*Accountable to None: The Tory Nationalisation of Britain*, 1995, p163)

Peter Hennessy notes a parallel and connected transformation in government with the growth of the select committees (*The Hidden Wiring*, 1995, pp152-60). These increasingly powerful bodies have widened their own terms of reference to include scrutiny of quangos. That move has created a whole new power circuit which by-passes party political debate and democracy, connecting up the farmed-out government functions of the quangos with an administrative committee structure. Now party political debate about the principles on which government acts can be completely side-stepped, while MPs on backroom select committees busy themselves checking the technical details of how the quangos disburse government funds and perform government functions.

The Labour Party has often attacked the quangos as wasteful and full of Tory placemen and women. But what is Labour's point? Is it asking for the quangos to be cut back, returning power to elected authorities, and for an end to political appointments? Not a bit of it. New Labour's complaint is that not enough of the sort of people it wants to see on these bodies are being appointed. Even Charter 88 and Democratic Audit do not propose to abolish the quangos outright, making the following, contradictory conclusion: 'The spread of EGOs [quangos] is a symptom of a systemic disease. The body politic itself has to be cured if they are to be brought under democratic control.' But if quangos are symptomatic of a systemic disease, then the answer is surely not to 'bring them under democratic control' but to root them out and get rid of them. Quangos have supplanted the democratic accountability of spending on urban development, health, education and social policy. The whole point of the quangos is that they are autonomous of democratic control, and for that reason 'non' or extra-governmental. For New Labour, however, democratic control of quangos appears to mean a more equal divide of the spoils between the parliamentary parties.

Indeed the Labour Party's plans for the House of Lords indicate that Labour sees a greater role for rule by appointment. You might have thought New Labour's preoccupation with constitutional reform would have led to a proposal to abolish the House of Lords or at least a move to curb its powers. But, while Labour does intend to reform the Lords, its principle concern is to make sure that this unelected body is stuffed with more of its kind of people. Labour wants to see more life peerages created among people who have 'contributed to the community'—code for people who share New Labour's values. This reform has been attacked by the Conservatives as the transformation of the lords into a giant quango—which would be a reasonable point but for the fact that the House of Lords, which the Tories support, already is a giant quango. The only debate between these two parties is over what kind of unelected dignitaries should exercise authority over us, blue bloods or do-gooders.

The prominent critics of Tory appointments policy are far from being champions of real democratic accountability. On the contrary, they denounce these bodies under the name of quangos, but celebrate similarly unelected and unaccountable organisations under the modified labels of 'non governmental organisations' (NGOs), the voluntary sector or community groups. Devolving more government authority to these is celebrated by the Labour Party as a 'multi-agency approach to social problems'.

The radical intelligentsia has in recent times softened its stance on quangos, as it comes to appreciate the potential virtues of side-stepping the vulgar electorate. So Geoff Mulgan claims that 'there is something to be gained from an agency focused on a task, and concentrated on its relationship with its key stakeholders, rather than a general purpose council that is [God forbid!] only account-able to the general electorate' (*What Needs to Change,* p225).

In Northern Ireland, where the electorate's continued support for the opposite poles of republicanism and Unionism has proved particularly frustrating for middle class reformers, the appeal of quangos is even clearer. Writing for the misnamed think tank Democratic Dialogue, John Morison argues that transferring government functions to quangos can provide an alternative to what he decries as 'all or nothing' democracy:

> Quangos are beyond the limits of constitutional control and so such a move may appear at first sight unequivocally undemocratic. But then the "constitutional control" of the increasingly moribund Westminster system is not itself entirely satisfactory. (*Democratic Dialogue,* No3)

In particular Morison thinks that quangos can give influence to those who have been 'disempowered under more "democratic" methods'. Presumably the scare quotation marks around the word democratic refer to the fact that nationalists in the North have been excluded from influence in Ulster through the extensive practice of gerrymandering and sectarianism. Until recently, however, opponents of that system had thought that more democracy not less was the solution and campaigned for equal rights and the unification of their country. From the perspective of Joseph Rowntree Trust-funded 'Democratic Dialogue', however, state patronage through quangos 'remains a potentially more democratic mechanism than a straightforward election in an unevenly divided and polarised society'. But then the six-county state in Northern Ireland has always been premised on the denial of democracy. What is new is that Morison's modern-day gerrymander-by-quango is a model not just for the suppression of democracy in Northern Ireland, but in Britain too.

WHO JUDGES THE JUDGES?

In October 1994 John Major established the Nolan Committee on Standards in Public Life after a series of scandals involving members of parliament. In particular, the committee was a response to the 'cash-for-questions' scandal, when MPs were said to have been paid to ask questions in parliament on behalf of lobbying companies. Lord Nolan and his colleagues 'quite deliberately' went beyond their terms of reference to set down a far-reaching set of proposals about how MPs' behaviour should be regulated, including the establishment of a Parliamentary Commissioner for Standards (see P Hennessy,

The Hidden Wiring, p181). In February 1996, the Scott commission reported on the arms-to-Iraq scandal, where, it was alleged, ministers had secretly relaxed guidelines on the sale of goods to Iraq, while at the same time telling parliament that no such adjustment had been made.

Both Nolan and Scott established an important precedent in the relationship between parliament and the judiciary. For the first time in years the judges were telling the politicians what they could and could not do. The balance of power between the elected legislature of MPs and the appointed judiciary was shifting.

Further evidence of the changes have come in a series of high-profile conflicts between the judges and the Tory Home Secretary Michael Howard. When the Chief Immigration Adjudicator Judge David Pearl overturned the deportation order issued against a Saudi dissident in the spring of 1996, it was Howard's ninth defeat at the hands of the courts in two years.

In March 1996 Britain's top judge, the then Lord Chief Justice, Lord Taylor, openly attacked a plan by the Home Secretary for fixed life sentences for a second violent offence. Clearly a Home Secretary who cannot bank on the support of his own Chief Justice is not in control of the criminal justice system. Clearly a Home Secretary who cannot serve a deportation order without it being overturned by a judge is not in control of immigration law. And, most importantly, a government that defers to justices Nolan and Scott in the matter of parliamentary conduct is not in control of parliament (see J Heartfield, 'Judges rule', and M Hume, 'Time to judge for ourselves', *Living Marxism,* April 1996).

In each recent case of a conflict between the judges and the Tory government it appears that it is the judges that stand for justice and liberty while the politicians are forcing through ever more draconian measures, from fixed sentences to summary deportations, as well as lying to the public and parliament. It is a traditional role that the judges have aspired to in the past, to defend liberty against the encroaching power of the state. And it is a role that has now made them more popular than they have been for a long time, as many of the Conservatives' critics look to the judiciary as the last bastion of freedom against a corrupt and dictatorial government.

But beneath the surface things are very different. The main motivating force behind the increased willingness of the judges to interfere in government decisions has little to do with defending our liberties. Judges like Lords Nolan and Taylor, or Sir Richard Scott are no friends of freedom. In the past they would not have been likely to break ranks with a Tory cabinet over small matters like misleading parliament and the public or doing dodgy arms deals or deporting Arabs. In fact judges have long been attuned to the need of the establishment to defend capitalist interests, even when that means riding roughshod over other people's liberties.

During his inquiry into the arms-to-Iraq affair, Sir Richard Scott won a media reputation as scourge of the Tory government, a radical in bicycle clips who would stand up for the public's right to know. Really? In 1984, when the *Guardian* newspaper leaked the siting of American nuclear Cruise missiles in Britain, the Ministry of Defence demanded to know who the mole was. Sir Richard Scott was the judge who ordered that the newspaper return the secret documents, so that the source could be discovered; as a result the young civil servant Sarah Tisdall was jailed for six months under the Official Secrets Act. It is ironic that Scott and his colleague Nolan are today seen as champions of the need to inform parliament and the public. Sarah Tisdall was afforded no such protection when she blew the whistle on how the Thatcher government was misleading MPs and the rest of us over its plans to install Cruise.

What is happening today is that the judges are trying to fill the vacuum caused by the government's crisis of legitimacy. The judiciary is particularly sensitive to the government's loss of authority. As that part of the state machinery which is entrusted with maintaining order, the judges are aghast at the extent to which the government has exposed the grubby shenanigans of capitalist rule to public ridicule and contempt. Instinctively, they are stepping in to shore up the legitimacy of the state—even if that means challenging the government of the day.

It is the collapsing authority of the elected legislature and the government that drives the conflict between the judges and the politicians. The judges, like nature, abhor a vacuum, and it is the power vacuum left by parliament that they are rushing to fill. Where uncertainty prevails, the judges want to see the rule of law restored to its former standing. Like the police chiefs, the judges, once fans of the Tories' law-and-order strategy are now less happy to be constantly in the front line of the government's increasingly hysterical clampdowns. What they fear is that their legitimacy will collapse alongside the government's, and so they are trying to establish some distance between them.

Most of the pretexts for the judicial challenge to parliament seem commonsensical. Arbitrary sentences and deportations, bribes and lies are hardly a sure basis on which to defend parliamentary sovereignty. Nonetheless the sum total of the judges activities are a further degradation of democracy, not a restoration of it. Politicians hold little favour with the public right now, but at least they are elected—not appointed by the government, acting in the name of the Crown, as the top three tiers of the judiciary are. If a ruling party offends you, you still have the right to throw them out of office. No such right obtains when it is the judges who are making the law. A senior judge can only be removed from office after motions have been passed by both houses of parliament. Little wonder that only *one* has been sacked in the 300 years since the rules were established, and that was back in 1830.

When the judiciary acts, it does not do so on behalf of liberty, but to shore up arbitrary and authoritarian power. The fact that this parliament is a sorry apology for a functioning democratic process should not blind us to the damaging consequences of allowing a greater role for judges in deciding the course of government. The principle of government by the people is even further dissipated if decisions are made by bewigged Lords drawn from the ruling classes. All the judges' authority stems from the dead weight of tradition, and all their criticisms are ranged against the presumed venality of mere elected politicians who have to play to the prejudices of the herd—that is, us.

Behind the judges' contempt for politicians is a contempt for the electorate. They do not trust ordinary people to decide the major questions of the day, any more than they trust the juries to judge the cases in their courts without hectoring and cajoling them. The judges instinctively mistrust the political process for its inconstancy and surprises. At root that mistrust is a distrust of popular decision-making.

Judicial intervention might seem to be a mechanism for bringing some kind of pressure on government to act in the people's interests. It is actually the very opposite. The greater role of the judges only formalises the exclusion of ordinary people from power.

THE EUROPEAN DIMENSION

One of the most important indicators of the perceived exhaustion of the 'Westminster model' is the growing importance of European political and governing institutions. Historically British politicians of all shades of opinion have viewed Europe with suspicion, jealously guarding the sovereignty of the Westminster parliament and the British judiciary. However, in more recent times a variety of oppositional forces in the UK have oriented themselves towards Europe in frustration with their inability to make a mark on Westminster. Institutions like the European Court of Human rights, the commissioners of the European Community and the European parliament have reciprocated this interest, providing an alternative focus for oppositional forces. Many oppositional forces have welcomed the European intervention as a powerful ally against the government. However, the intrusion of unaccountable European institutions has only reinforced the degradation of British democracy.

In recent years, all of the movements and lobbies in the UK that have found their ambitions frustrated at Westminster have taken their cause to Europe. Since the eighties, the Scottish Nationalists have embraced 'the European dimension' as a possible solution to two problems: the continued rule of a 'colonial' Tory government in Westminster, and the lack of credibility of the nationalist arguments for an economically viable independent Scotland.

Nationalists in Northern Ireland, frustrated by British and Unionist intransigence, were the next to see the possibilities of Europe. In 1993 the Opsahl commission, which was fronted by former European Commissioner for Human Rights, Torkel Opsahl, gave a degree of legitimacy to their complaints that was not forthcoming from Westminster. The European Court of Human Rights' decision that the SAS execution of three IRA volunteers in Gibraltar in 1988 was unlawful increased the expectation that European institutions would be more open to nationalist concerns.

The British trade union movement has for most of its existence been hostile to Europe, favouring import controls against European goods and opposing European union in the seventies and early eighties. However, the exclusion of the trade unions from government circles under the Conservatives has driven the TUC to look again at the advantages of getting European institutions involved When then EC commissioner Jacques Delors launched the Social Chapter, a raft of minimal employment rights which the British government opted out of, he provided a new focus for TUC lobbying. When Delors, the Tories' *bête noire,* addressed the British Trade Union Congress in 1988, he was given a standing ovation.

For Britain's radical middle classes, too, Europe seemed to hold out the promise of reform where the Conservative monopoly on power did not. Charter 88, the constitutional reform movement quickly saw the advantage of Europe as an alternative focus of power. At the top of its list of political priorities, Charter 88 aims 'to get the European Convention on Human Rights incorporated into British law' (*Prospects and Plans for the Nineties,* 1990), a move that Lord Lestor attempted in the House of Lords last year. Civil rights organisations have also made European institutions a focus of campaigning, as have campaigners on issues ranging from the rights of asylum-seekers to homosexual equality.

The appeal of Europe to all of the marginalised forces in British society has been that it appears to offer an arena of change where Westminster does not. An important part of this appeal is the fact that pursuing the European option means sidestepping the problem of winning popular support for change in Britain. Westminster is unattractive because it sets the test of winning over public opinion at the polls. These forces are not so much disappointed with the institution of parliament as with the task of convincing the majority. For many oppositional movements, the European dimension appeals because it avoids the need to win an argument and support among the people, and offers an escape root for movements reaching a dead-end. For the Scottish nationalists Europe meant that they could put aside the question of an independent Scotland's credibility. For the nationalists of Northern Ireland, internationalising the conflict meant 'transcending' the national question without realising national independence. For the radical intelligentsia in Charter 88, and for the trade unions, European institutions were an authority that could bully the unyielding Conservative government.

As a solution that excused oppositional movements the onerous task of securing public support, it was implicit that turning to Europe would lead further away from democracy. For, despite the often more liberal face of European institutions, the extension of their writ in the United Kingdom is profoundly undemocratic. This is a lesson that radical critics are unwilling to learn, since they hear the argument for parliamentary sovereignty abused in the defence of Conservative policy. All the same, the extension of European legislation and adjudication into Britain offers no extension of popular choice and only removes the centres of power further from the people.

In substance, the European Convention on Human Rights offers little prospect of a more liberal regime. Its articles are in every instance so hedged about with qualifications as to make them even more restrictive than existing British law. On freedom of speech, for example, exceptions on grounds of national security, decency, public health and so on make the 'right' a nonsense. The European Court seems to offer hope, but its judges are no more responsive to truly popular control than are the judges in Britain. Similarly the provisions of the Social Chapter are minimal, conceived only as a sop to soften the blow of the pro-market policies enshrined in the Maastricht agreement.

Most pointedly, though, the European option moves power away from the people. The judges of the European Court, the Commissioners of the EC and the Council of Ministers act outside of any popular control or accountability. These European institutions are closely entwined with the monopoly of power held by the ruling elites of the continent. Today the authority of the governing institutions of Europe only provides a reserve of power for a British state that does not enjoy popular support. Any movement for real democracy would have to include the demand to get unaccountable European institutions out of public affairs, just as much as opposing the power of the quangos and the judges.

DEMOCRACY AND THE QUESTION OF POWER

The exhaustion of the British political process has led to all kinds of questions being asked about how we are governed, questions that once would have seemed like treason. The near-sacred role of the monarchy has been well and truly undermined. And the sanctity of British parliamentary democracy has been questioned in terms that would have been taboo in the recent past.

Alongside the empty debate between the political parties, there is now an increasingly important second debate about reforming the system of government itself. This discussion has been driven by a variety of radical groups and critical voices in society, including the campaign for a written constitution and bill of rights, Charter 88, the left-of-centre think-tanks, the Institute for Public Policy Research and Demos, the Labour-backed Social Justice Commission and a range of pressure groups like Liberty, Justice, Greenpeace, Amnesty International, the campaigning arm of the Body Shop and the World Development Movement.

These critics all point out how the two-party system is failing to reflect the desires and aspirations of ordinary people, or to defend civil liberties, or to provide a framework for effective government. Most avow their intention to improve democracy. But without exception all the reforms proposed tend to subordinate the rule of the people to government by appointed authorities.

Many commentators have become less convinced by the virtues of representative democracy. Indeed they increasingly see it as an anachronism, dismissing it variously by the addition of such qualifiers as 'all-or-nothing' democracy, 'first-past-the-post' democracy, the 'Westminster model', 'majoritarianism', 'parliamentary sovereignty' or 'elective dictatorship'. What all these terms have in common is that they identify the proper meaning of democracy, majority rule, as if it was in fact a perversion of democracy.

It is one of the peculiarities of the debate about governing institutions that the critique of democracy is usually conducted in the name of democracy, even of widening democracy and democratic participation. In that way the various radical critics lay claim to the 'true meaning' of democracy. But that should not confuse us. In every instance, the various critics conflate their own narrow concerns with the spirit of democracy. The central theme of the debate is that representative democracy is at best redundant and at worst a cover for dictatorship.

CHECKS AND BALANCES

In his essay *Citizens and Subjects* Labour MP and Charter 88 supporter Tony Wright takes issue with the British parliamentary system, by way of a critique of the constitutional expert AV Dicey, the proponent of the doctrine of 'parliamentary sovereignty':

> Dicey had made democracy too easy, and too simple. Without knowing it, or liking it, he had provided a view of the constitution which enabled democracy to become a matter of political parties claiming mandates to rule on the basis of electoral (or, more precisely, parliamentary) majorities, in a context where the restraints on ruling were meagre and informal. (1994, p2)

This is an interesting statement. The proposition that seems so questionable to Wright—parties claiming mandates from the electorate—has, after all, been the staple of Britain's claim to be a democracy for the last 300 years. What is more, the short-comings Wright sees in this set-up, the lack of restraints on ruling, are a new concern for someone from the left of centre. Traditionally, it has been conservatives who sought checks on elective power and a balanced constitution, in their desire to hold back the tide of popular democracy. How is it that someone who purports to embrace democracy should end up repeating Lord Hailsham's charge against democracy that it led to an 'elective dictatorship'?

Anyone listening to Tony Wright, or the Real World Coalition, or Charter 88 could be forgiven for thinking that there was one profound change taking place in the organisation of British social and political life: the overweening concentration of power in the hands of the executive. But these activists are blind to the fact that they are proposing another anti-democratic transformation of the system. Like somebody filling out an accident insurance claim they can only see the movement of the other vehicle, unaware that they were the ones making an unconventional manoeuvre. Their critique of Britain's governing institutions reflects the real passage away from parliamentary sovereignty and towards the various, novel forms of official regulation described above, whether the law lords or Europe. Far from it being the case that the country is in the grip of an 'elective dictatorship', parliament is increasingly side-stepped by the judiciary and by the unelected quangos that dictate so much of public expenditure. And these infringements of democracy are being made by the very forces that are championed by the radical critics of the parliamentary system of government.

POWER UNDER QUESTION

For hundreds of years conservatives and reactionaries have sought a 'separation of powers' under a 'balanced constitution'. Their goal was to keep political power dispersed among different arms of the state, from the Crown to the judiciary to the houses of parliament. As they saw it, the separation of powers would mean that authority could not easily be challenged. The balanced constitution would be a barrier to popular sovereignty. If the mass of people exercised too great an influence on any one arm of the state, like the parliament or the army, they could still be denied overall control by the other instruments of state power. This conservative principle has long been the last line of defence for elitism against popular power. But, surprisingly, it has recently become the staple of the radical critique of democracy, too.

The central issue in the debate about Britain's governing institutions is that of power. Power centralised in the hands of the executive, say these critics must tend towards dictatorship, echoing Lord Acton's dictum 'power corrupts, and absolute power corrupts absolutely'. The vast weight of the reforms proposed are towards the diffusion of power across many institutions, and the restraint of power, through constitutional reform. According to Labour leader Tony Blair 'devolving power and democratising power is an idea whose time has come' (*What Needs to Change,* p14).

So Tony Wright calls for a 'disaggregation of representation away from over-arching structures where it is least effective and into new structures for particular functions and services (for example policing, education or health) where it is most effective' (*Citizens and Subjects,* p97). But the claims of 'representation' were never simply what is effective, but what is the will of the people. Reduced to a question of technical efficiency, no doubt there is a case for seeing decision-making broken up along lines of function or profession. But democracy demands that all priorities are open to national debate.

The Labour Party, though, has little instinct for democracy, for all its talk of reform. New Labour's proposals for the monarchy, in wanting to see royalty reformed instead of executed, fall short of those of the parliament of 1649. Similarly its proposals for the

House of Lords would entrench this unelected second chamber, by the appointment of new life peerages. For anyone with an ounce of democratic principle the solution to both these aristocratic institutions should be obvious—abolition. However, in substance, New Labour is broadly sympathetic to the idea that there should be other centres of state power outside of a democratically elected parliament. Cringing to the Queen or waiting for a minor upset for the government in the Lords seems to appeal to the Labour front bench. They have always hoped to exercise authority by the good grace of the powers that be more than they have ever trusted the ordinary mass of people.

In this discussion the very meaning of the word 'democracy' has been redefined. Increasingly democracy is taken to mean nothing more than the diffusion of power to a variety of different governing institutions, whether the judiciary, devolved regional assemblies and local government, European institutions, or the non-governmental organisations. So, for example, the Real World Coalition argues that 'political power needs to be diffused, both upwards and downwards' and further, that 'the European Union is the essential starting point, since it already has powers' (*The Politics of the Real World,* p112). The coalition sees the downward diffusion of power as meaning the increased role and authority of NGOs, which is to say, of radical quangos.

The critics find it easy to describe the symptoms of the problem, to demonstrate how the failure of the party political system already means that political power is exercised arbitrarily, often unjustly and with little restraint. However, their conclusions represent less of a solution to the problem, than its natural progression towards the closure of popular participation in decision-making. Instead of putting power in the hands of the people, they favour the disaggregation of power through a complex array of unaccountable institutions—quangos, the courts, European bodies and so on.

Once opposition movements had a very different estimate of the question of power. State power could be a force for progressive reform, as much as it could be an instrument of repression in the hands of the ruling class. The political strategy of the left was not the diffusion, but the seizure of power, so that it could be deployed for the good of all. The relative democratisation of the state in the twentieth century reinforced the appeal of this programme, as it was seen that mass support could be mobilised in favour of progressive social reform.

Today's alternative programme for the diffusion of political power reflects the disappointment of opposition forces not only in the programme of state reform, but also in the willingness of the masses to support it. Having failed to convince a majority of their cause, they turn their backs on the contest for public opinion in favour of 'disaggregating majorities' and 'diffusing power'.

AVOIDING THE FIGHT

It is significant that the notion of diffusing power really took off after the Labour Party lost its third general election in a row in 1987, and strengthened after Labour's fourth consecutive defeat in 1992. Every time radical activists had taken a programme of variously strong and weak reform to the voters in election campaigns, the left was rejected in favour of a Conservative government. Rather than seeing the voters as potential allies to be won over to a fight for change, radicals began to resent the inordinate and obstructive influence of the working classes upon the organisation of government. Resenting the political authority of the Conservative government, they took at face value the claim that this authority derived from the people.

Labour MP Michael Meacher, once a fellow traveller of the hard left gave a particularly clear version of the argument for restraining representative democracy in favour of the dispersal of power in his book *Diffusing Power: The Key to Socialist Renewal* published in 1992 in the wake of Labour's fourth election defeat. There he painted a picture of the dictatorial power of elected government as a barrier to the strategies of the left: 'Thatcher's aggressive pursuit of "authoritarian populism" certainly played an important role in demoralising opposition to what would otherwise have been seen as her unacceptable extremism.' (p12) Beneath the name-calling this is not so much a rejection of Thatcher as a rejection of 'populism', or the choice of the people. As he glumly observes, 'her slogan of "power to the people" carried a resonance beyond her traditional bailiwick'.

At this point, any self-respecting radical ought surely to redouble their efforts to claim the slogan 'power to the people' for their own project. But not the newly chastened champion of the Labour left. Instead Meacher insists that 'Thatcher's themes should not be copied' and takes succour from the fact that 'resentment became widespread at the whole idea of elective dictatorship and over-mighty government'. Meacher is dismayed that 'the fundamental British doctrine of the separation of powers was...under threat' (p12).

Had people like Michael Meacher the insight or honesty to understand that it was their own programme that was deficient, not the voters' understanding of it, they might have drawn very different conclusions about the question of power. But blaming the voters for embracing the 'authoritarian populism' of Margaret Thatcher instead, radicals began unconsciously to reorient their attitude towards power. Now, instead of seeing political power as a tool to be seized centrally, radicals worked out strategies to share power behind the backs of the electorate. Now the left came to see the centralisation of power as a barrier rather than a boon to change.

REGULATING DEMOCRACY

All the pet projects of political reform embraced by radical critics of the Tory government side-step the question of a contest for popular support. Charter 88 was the first major campaign to aim for the diffusion of power as a goal, favouring the independence of the judiciary, the creation of regional assemblies and the constraint of government through a written constitution and bill of rights. The ostensible claim was to regenerate British democracy. But in content this was a programme to get around the unwelcome choice made by the electorate. Without recourse to a popular mandate, these radicals looked instead to unelected authorities, like the judges and the European court to achieve the results that the voters had denied them. Charter 88 became a model campaign for the diffusion of political power, and a blue-print for the elevation of officialdom over democratic choice. Its demands for the independence of the judiciary, for proportional representation, for constitutional restraint on the choice of the voters had little to do with the classical conception of democracy as the rule of the people, but rather reproduced the old conserv-ative demands for a 'balanced constitution' with a system of 'checks and balances'.

In its assessment of the standing of democracy, the think-tank Demos finds parliamentary procedure wanting. Decrying parliament as a mere talking shop, Demos goes on to outline the kind of changes that it thinks would increase democracy. In practice each of these is a constraint on the already attenuated character of representation. They include such things as voter juries and deliberative polling groups, constituent's charters and electronic polling. But all of these gadgets confuse the very nature of representation.

> Our current system seems particularly archaic and peculiarly resis-tant to rich and modulated communication from voters to politicians. On election days, modern citizens come home from offices crammed full of computers, faxes and digital phone systems, to homes almost equally cluttered with telephones and videos, and on the way vote by scribbling a cross on pieces of paper which are then put into wooden boxes. (*Lean Democracy,* Demos Quarterly, p7)

To which one can only say, 'and a good job too'. The idea that elections should become part of the moronic inferno of video entertainment and office technology would be too much to bear. It is quite bad enough that we have to suffer the inanities of the established political parties without being obliged to engage in the 'rich and modulated communication' of stuttering and unreadable fax machines, endlessly downloading Internet programmes and, horror of horrors, telephone polling, just to have a say. It is strange that intelligent people could so comprehensively misunderstand the political process as to think that it was a matter of the *technology* of communication, rather than its *substance*.

Of course, if representation really were put into a framework of new technology that would delimit the character of representation on class lines. Noam Chomsky recently attacked the Internet as a world elite. Something of an over-reaction, and a bad judgement to boot, since it could only mean surrendering this new technology to the elites. Nonetheless he does have a point, in that new technologies tend to be monopolised by those with the means to pay for them and the leisure time to invest in them. An electronic democracy would be an unrepresentative one.

Demos is not the only organisation that confuses the paraphernalia of marking the ballot paper with the substance of democracy, that is making real decisions about how things should be. The Rock the Vote Campaign has dedicated itself to countering voter 'apathy' especially among the young. On the model of the successful voter registration campaign that preceded the American election in 1992, Rock the Vote aims to use the influence of pop stars to persuade young people to put themselves on the electoral register. On the face of things, countering young people's disengagement from politics is an admirable goal. However, the Rock the Vote campaign makes the mistake of thinking that the problem is apathy among the young, rather than the exhaustion of the old politics (see B Waterfield, 'What will voting rock?', *Living Marxism*, April 1996).

Rock the Vote campaigners proudly proclaim that their campaign is not affiliated to any political party and its aim is to get people voting, whatever party they vote for. As they see it, you have no right to criticise if you do not vote. But the reason that younger people are not voting is that there is no real choice between the main parties. The problem is not apathy among the young, but the crisis of political leadership presented by the main parties. In the absence of a real choice, what is voting for? At the most it could be an exercise in civic responsibility—which is what the Rock the Vote campaign represents. When Noel Gallagher lauded Tony Blair at the 1996 Brit Awards it was no more plausible than the sight of Virginia Bottomley grooving on down at the back of the hall. This cynical exercise in educating the young indicates contempt for their opinions rather than respect.

Demos also advocates an audit of parliament. So, too, does the constitutional historian and Labour Party adviser Peter Hennessy, who regrets that cabinet ministers were excluded from the independent audit of Whitehall instigated by Mrs Thatcher (see *The Hidden Wiring*). In the Demos publication *Lean Democracy* Martin Summers makes the following assessment of parliament: 'Its introverted culture is exacerbated by the absence of any systems of accountability found elsewhere in the public and private sectors.' (p10) But parliament is accountable—accountable to the electorate. For Summers, though, the assumption that elections are 'sufficient' 'is not easily sustainable when most MPs have safe seats' (p12). It seems to be inconceivable to Summers that the reason why Tory and Labour MPs have safe seats is that thousands of people continue to vote for them because nobody has put forward a viable political alternative to the parties which they stand for. On the contrary, Summers is entirely ignorant of the fact that people vote for MPs on the basis of their political programmes. He wants to see MPs audited for their attendance in the chamber and on the ubiquitous select committees. To enforce these procedural priorities, Summers advocates a constituent's charter.

The real content of these reforms could only be that the people's elected representatives would be subordinate to yet another ombudsman or regulatory body that audited MPs on their performance, with all the interest in political representation that a time-and-motion man has in what is being produced. Of course, in real terms there already is a supra-parliamentary audit of MPs, and that is the Nolan commission: the first step towards the anti-democratic regulation of parliament.

FOR THE TYRANNY OF THE MAJORITY

Michael Meacher argues that the answer to the concentration of power is to be found in the ideas of Karl Marx (at least those that he does not think have been superseded by events):

where the Marxist model still points the way is in identifying the locus of power as the key criterion distinguishing a capitalist society from a socialist society, and in insisting that a central facet of socialism lies in mobilising the mass of the people to throw off or abolish the source of power used by a minority to exploit the majority. (*Diffusing Power*, p14)

Which is very well put, but for one important omission. To abolish the current concentration of political power, the mass of people will need to seize that power for themselves, to deploy it against the exploiting minority. Marx's case was not for the diffusion of power, but for the 'dictatorship of the proletariat', the forcible suppression of the minority of the property-owning elite at the hands of the majority, as the first step towards the creation of a free and equal society.

Far from being a barrier to social change, the concentration of power is its precondition. That proposition seems perverse to the radical critics of the Conservative government because of the reactionary ends to which political power is put today. But refusing to fight for political authority must necessarily surrender it to reaction (see J Heartfield, 'For the tyranny of the majority', *Living Marxism*, February 1996).

The 'diffusion of power' seems to be a more sensitive, less dangerous option than concentrating it in one place. But nothing could be further from the truth. In fact, the 'diffusion of power' is not a distant objective, but a real condition of today. Political power is already being diffused. That is exactly what the process of disaggregating parliamentary democracy in favour of the rule of judges, the quangocracy and the Brussels bureaucrats is—the 'diffusion of power'.

This sort of diffused power is, as Lord Acton understood when he first proposed a separation of powers, a barrier to the united action of the majority. Elites have always sought refuge in the diffusion of political power, because that diffuseness removes any question of who rules from open discussion and debate. However, nobody should think that the diffusion of political power means that real power is not being exercised by an elite. The domination of society by capital, and those who own and control it, is not challenged by the diffusion of political power. On the contrary, frustrating the organisation of political majorities in society is the key to the otherwise untenable rule of the capitalists. A society which gives precedence to minorities over majorities in the name of democracy will always be prey to the power of that most undemocratic of minorities, the capitalist elite.

The process of undermining democracy in favour of a modern-day separation of powers is much advanced. Already a sixth of the state's resources are deployed by unelected quangos. Already parliament is regulated by and regularly overruled by unelected judges. Open debate in parliament is being downgraded in favour of the committee room deliberations of self-appointed experts. More than ever before, the electorate is reduced to the role of stage army in a non-contest between interchangeable parties. These developments are a degradation of democracy, but they are celebrated as its renewal by the government's radical critics. In substance, they are the guarantee of the continuing dictatorship of capital over society. Fighting for democratic power against the new and old generations of authoritarians alike is a precondition of imposing the rule of the majority and changing the way in which society is organised. It is not a question of either defending or amending constitutional traditions, but of upholding the right of the people to determine their own destiny.

THE MORALS OF CAUTION

6

The 'precautionary principle', or what we might call the morality of risk-avoidance, is as dangerous and repressive as Victorian values were in times gone by.

One theme that runs through much of what we have discussed so far is the powerful sense of uncertainty that prevails today, the feeling that people can no longer take anything very much for granted. There is no longer an agreed set of values in society. So, for example, every time another expert emerges to insist that children must be taught the difference between right and wrong, it only serves to raise the question of what 'right' and 'wrong' really mean today on any issue from sexual practices to farming methods. One consequence of this uncertainty has been to encourage all manner of attempts to reimpose some kind of moral order on society—an effort which has created many more problems than it has solved.

The dictum that politicians pronounce on morality at their own peril has been well illustrated in recent years. Soon after Conservative prime minister John Major announced a policy of 'Back to basics'—a return to basic moral values—his party and his cabinet was engulfed in sexual and financial scandals. Social security minister Peter Lilley's moral crusades against single mothers for 'scrounging' off the welfare state have proved equally unsuccessful.

To many people, politicians pontificating on moral matters only make themselves look like hypocrites, demanding that others do as they say, not as they do. The bogus sermonising of politicians tends to deplete the authority of moral claims, reducing these to cheap tricks designed to win political advantage. What purports to be a universal moral standard is revealed as nothing more than the sectional interests of a power-hungry party.

Nonetheless, politicians seem keener than ever to clothe themselves in purple and deliver moral sermons, especially on the opposition benches. So Tony Blair has said that Christianity is the basis of his political beliefs. David Blunkett has called for a return to the teaching of basic moral values in schools. John Major's comment that we should understand a little less and condemn a little more would hardly be out of place on Labour's front bench. Labour home affairs spokesman Paul Boateng wants the American law-enforcement practice of 'Zero tolerance' adopted in Britain, and, in an alarming return to the seventeenth century, advocates 'summary justice'.

Setting aside the considerations of party political advantage, there is good reason for the current fascination with morality in politics. Both the desire of politicians to pronounce on morality and their failure to secure moral agreement are expressions of a real problem—the absence of a moral consensus in society.

Active membership of mainstream Christian churches has fallen dramatically in the past 20 years even though Britain already has the lowest church participation in Europe, just 15 per cent of the population in 1990 (compared to 81 per cent in Ireland). According to researcher Lynn Revell, mainstream Christian belief has declined markedly, while interest in New Age religious beliefs has grown (see 'Return of the Sacred', *Marxism, Mysticism and Modern Theory*, 1996). This has led to the Church of England adapting to New Age rituals and services, occasionally with unanticipated consequences, such as the scandal over Chris Brain's ministry in Sheffield, where a 'New Age' congregation fell apart amid allegations of sexual and financial impropriety.

According to Revell, faith now tends to rest more upon the privately held beliefs of the individual than a moral consensus expressed in church doctrine. The idea of your own personal faith is much stronger than collective religious observance today. Dr Johnson long since expressed the conservative's dilemma with this kind of personal faith, observing that the trouble with a man who is guided by an inner light is that you do not know where to find him.

The lack of a moral consensus presents a major problem for the authorities in their desire to maintain a stable social order. Even in a country as relaxed in its religious outlook as Britain, moralism has been a mainstay of the status quo, injecting a powerful conservatism into society. Moral constraints have moderated oppositional movements and provided the glue that holds society together, underpinning the basic stability that the ruling elite relies upon. In the nineteenth century both Methodism and Catholicism acted as moderating forces upon the growing working class as the chapel and the mass helped to counter the Chartist meeting and the trades union. In the 1980s government supporters called for a return to 'Victorian values' as a counter to the supposed influence of the 'loony left' on social issues. Though there is little organised opposition to the ruling elite from the labour movement or the left today, the sense of social breakdown is profound, and anxieties over the lack of common values abound.

But perhaps even more important than the imagined dangers of social breakdown is the sense of moral confusion within the establishment itself. Without a clear and unchallengeable set of beliefs in common, the ruling elite finds itself unable to act in unison. For the Conservative government this problem is profound. On many occasions the government has called upon the church to assume moral leadership in the country. But to the Conservatives' consternation, the church has proved unwilling to deliver a clear and unambiguous viewpoint on the superiority of heterosexuality, marriage and obedience. The Archbishop of Canterbury, while condemning 'moral relativism' and political corruption in a major speech in July 1996, later declined to denounce the adultery practised by a future 'defender of the faith', Prince Charles. Similarly, the government has found it difficult to agree a common position on sentencing with the judges, and on punishment with the prison and probation services.

This moral confusion and uncertainty within the establishment is one reason why so many at the top are willing to believe the worst about wider society. Unsure of their own ability to do the right thing, they feel confident that the rest of us must be rapidly descending into depravity. Consequently many of their fears about social breakdown and desperate demands for 'community' underestimate the ability of most people to get on with their lives without the moral strictures of a priesthood. The elites project their own insecurities on to the rest of us. All the same, the failure to secure a clear moral consensus is a profound disadvantage for the establishment.

ETHICS MAN

The problems of faith and certainty have led to a renewed interest in matters of ethics and morality: business ethics, medical ethics and so on. An academic school of moral philosophy has grown into an influential body of thought. According to philosopher Alasdair MacIntyre, modern society operates as if there were an agreed set of values, but on enquiry finds that there is no such thing. MacIntyre identifies the new interest in, and funding for, 'applied ethics' in universities as a response to this problem. He sees the rise of applied ethics, not as a 'genuine moral enquiry', but an attempt to grapple with practical problems in the professional lives of doctors, lawyers, accountants and corporate executives:

> Every such profession cannot dispense with a code defining appropriate behaviour both between professional and client and between professional and professional. The acute need felt in the last 20 years to refurbish these codes has had two distinct sources. One is the degree of change in the issues requiring professional decisions, in medicine often the result of technological innovation; the other is the poverty of the shared morality of liberal, pluralist societies and its consequent resourcelessness to provide what the professions have needed. (*Three Rival Versions of Moral Enquiry*, 1990, p226)

In recent years the growth of concern with ethics has indeed been profound; see, for instance, the flourishing of government-sponsored inquiries into things like the ethics of *in vitro* fertilisation, animal-to-human transplants and fertility treatment for the post-menopausal woman. Furthermore, these inquiries have laid down codes and rules, but have not established a universal moral consensus. Instead their by-words are caution in research and caution in definitive moral statements.

Novelist and philosopher Iris Murdoch, endorsing MacIntyre's prognosis has pointed to the absence of a sure basis for moral belief in modern societies. In her *Metaphysics as a Guide to Morals* she writes that: 'We yearn for the transcendent, for God, for something divine and good and pure, but in picturing the transcendent we transform it into idols which we then realise to be contingent particulars, just things among others here below.' (1992, p56) Murdoch is bemoaning society's apparent inability to repair the failure of moral certainty. The various attempts by politicians of left and right to assert by diktat a morality of 'Back to basics', or one based on the values of 'community', are, she suggests, bound to fail. Attempts to impose a set of universal moral values will invariably fall apart in the face of disagreement. What purports to be the general good will be exposed as the narrow interests of a particular section of society.

We noted in an earlier chapter how the Conservative government had been unnerved to discover that its traditional moralism had little purchase on our complex modern society. Perhaps most disturbing for the capitalists is the view among moral philosophers that the values of free market individualism are themselves to blame for disrupting moral order. According to this argument, the enterprising individual of market theory necessarily lacks concern for the wider community, putting himself before anyone else. This kind of atomism, it is argued, leads to conflict, crime and despair (see C Taylor, *Sources of the Self*, 1989). The attack on individualism and self-interest seems to be a particularly bitter blow to the ideologues of the free market.

However, despite the difficulties encountered in artificially creating a moral order, or the perceived conflict between the market and morality, there is nonetheless an emerging moralism that is more appropriate for our times. Its emergence is helping the authorities to fill the gap left by the crumbling of traditional values, and lend some sense of consensus to contemporary society. This is what we might call the morality of risk-avoidance, or what is often called the 'precautionary principle'. And it is as dangerous and repressive as right-wing Victorian values were in times gone by.

AVOIDING RISK

The morality of risk-avoidance was well illustrated by the great mad cow panic of 1996. As we have already noted, there was no firm evidence at all to support the thesis of a link between BSE and CJD. Once the beef panic was introduced into the public domain, however, no amount of official blandishment could disturb the perception of danger. Television and newspapers sought the Consumers' Association's response to the beef scare as a non-partisan voice in the dispute. The only way to be absolutely safe, the CA said, was to avoid beef altogether. It was an interesting remark. The Consumers' Association readily admitted that no link had been proved. But that was not the point. If there was even a potential that beef might present a risk, then the only way to avoid that risk was to avoid beef.

Risk-avoidance is, as we saw in Chapter Two, a prevailing preoccupation of our times. It draws upon the overwhelming perception of danger that has soured contemporary living. But the sense of risk is more than just a sentiment. It is increasingly a moderating influence upon our behaviour, in a way that no religious or civic authority could hope to be today. Increasingly doctors and other experts and authorities are replacing priests, and are being taken seriously as guides to good behaviour and worthy living (see F Füredi, 'The dangers of safety', *Living Marxism,* July/August 1996).

According to the government survey *Social Trends,* for example, there have been marked changes over the past 30 years in the type of food British households eat. They note that 'Doctors advise eating less fats containing saturated fatty acids, to avoid high levels of cholesterol in the blood and the risk of heart disease'. And, 'as a result' of this advice 'there has been a switch in household consumption from butter, firstly towards margarine and more recently to low and reduced fat spreads'. Also, 'the average person drinks less milk today than in 1961'. And as for meat...the amount of carcase beef and lamb (ie, excluding meat products) we eat has generally fallen over the last 30 years. In 1992 each person ate, on average, under five ounces of beef and veal per week, only about half the amount consumed in 1961. Lamb and mutton consumption has fallen more sharply; the average amount consumed in 1992 had dropped to almost a third of the figure 30 years ago. (*Social Trends,* 1994, p98)

What is remarkable is the authority which health experts now exercise over our diet. Britain has not been known before for its observance of dietary laws. The Church of England never really had the authority of more diligently observed religions, and could not dictate what went on in the kitchen as Islam or Judaism did. But if Britons are unmoved by any religious dietary laws, there is one kind of observance to which even the nationality known as *rosbifs* for their eating habits are susceptible these days, and that is the observance of personal health and safety.

In the name of personal health and safety, many of us are willing to accept the kind of strictures that would seem intrusive or moralistic if they came from a more traditional figure of authority. The fascinating thing about 'risk-avoidance' is that it creates a contemporary kind of morality that does not seem to be a morality at all. Where not many people are willing to obey God's rules without question, or indeed the rules of law-abiding and pluralistic society, the rules of risk-avoidance appear to be compelling. The safety precautions laid down today go far beyond simple procedures of a technical nature, to advocate specific kinds of interpersonal behaviour. However, they do so in such a way as to leave their moral content unannounced. What are in fact moral strictures seem to be entirely innocent— a commonsensical presentation of nothing more than good health tips or a practical guide to staying safe. The contemporary rules of risk-avoidance disguise moralising as personal safety.

THE EXAMPLE OF AIDS-AWARENESS

'AIDS-awareness' and 'safer sex' are the models for contemporary risk-avoidance. Spending on AIDS in Britain by the NHS and local authorities stands at £285m a year (*Britain 1996: An Official Handbook,* HMSO, 1996). That would mean £82 000 spent on each of the 3480 people suffering from AIDS, an admirably humane policy—except that the vast bulk of the money is not spent upon AIDS sufferers at all. Most expenditure is not on care or even cure, but on AIDS education. (Similarly some £40m a year is spent on 'drug prevention' and £3m a year on alcohol treatment. Again, most of this money is not spent curing disease, but advocating certain kinds of behaviour and discouraging others.)

Is AIDS-awareness really about health? No. Ten years of hard statistics have proven the analysis which *Living Marxism* writers put forward from the start of the AIDS panic: that, in the West, AIDS is extremely difficult to contract outside of the recognised high-risk groups—gay men, intravenous drug-users and people from the Third World. After a decade of officially sponsored scaremongering about the threat of AIDS to everyone, there is no evidence that HIV infection is a problem for the heterosexual population. Over the entire course of the epidemic up to early 1996, just 161 people, who were not members of the high-risk groups or their sexual partners, had developed AIDS in the UK (see Centre for Disease Surveillance and Control, *Communicable Disease Report,* Vol6 No16, 19 April 1996). Yet the non-appearance of the long-predicted explosion of AIDS within the heterosexual population has not dampened the enthusiasm of the authorities for pushing 'AIDS-awareness' programmes. (And the one thing which we can be sure these programmes do not make people 'aware' of is that most of them have about as much chance of developing AIDS as they have of winning the national lottery.)

Local authorities, health authorities and schools promote specific models of sexual behaviour under the cover of educating people about risks to their health. The content of a typical AIDS lesson seems to be non-committal on moral behaviour, but the underlying message is clear. According to the many Health Education Authority leaflets, students should first be asked to identify the risks of AIDS and what kind of acts can lead to HIV infection. Then you might encourage them to act out a boy-meets-girl scenario. Discussion should concentrate on whether both partners are prepared emotionally to cope with sex: have they talked about it? Are they responding to peer pressure?

Through the discussion of the risks of AIDS, young people are being tutored in proper sexual behaviour in a way that they would be unlikely to accept from a vicar. What would be the likely response if a school student were to say that the danger of an AIDS epidemic had been massively exaggerated? It is unlikely that a rational discussion of the actual incidence of AIDS would ensue. More likely the miscreant would be denounced for his 'ignorance'. What reception would a teenager face who admitted that he did not use a condom during sex? It would be difficult to call it anything but moral opprobrium. Pupils are encouraged to resist pressure from their peers, but how are they to resist the pressure from AIDS-awareness?

The trick behind AIDS-awareness training is that morality is reposed as personal safety. Nobody could be in favour of infecting themselves with HIV. So it follows that we must all do what is necessary to avoid infection. However, the dangers of contracting AIDS are minute, for all but a few people in high-risk groups— most of whom are well serviced by dedicated advisory and support networks. Indeed America's top AIDS agency, the Centre for Disease Control, has admitted that it has been exaggerating the likely incidence of AIDS outside the high-risk groups for years, with the express purpose of keeping AIDS in the public mind (see *Wall Street Journal,* 1 May 1996).

Author Molly Parkin recalls a scene from her Welsh valley childhood where at chapel the vicar giving the sermon asked all the women in the congregation to cross their legs. 'And now the gates of hell are firmly shut', he said, 'I will begin'. Today not even the most devout conservative would dare to identify sexuality with eternal damnation so pointedly. But the message of AIDS-awareness carries a similar emotional weight. Sexual indiscretion will lead to a lingering death from AIDS. The connection between sin and damnation could hardly be more explicit. As with religion, we are all potential sinners, or in modern terms all potentially at risk. Furthermore we must all exercise constant vigilance, or in modern terms, AIDS-awareness and safer sex.

The connection between personal hygiene and moral behaviour is not entirely new. In *The Anxiety Makers: Some Curious Preoccupations of the Medical Profession,* Alex Comfort describes the many ways that young people around the turn of the century were threatened with dementia and blindness if they engaged in masturbation or excessive fornication. Doubtless doctors then were as sincere about the risks they imagined would flow from onanism as they are today about AIDS. But the imagined threat of 'disease' showed the way that morality was increasingly being represented in the secular form of a medical 'science'.

Such scare stories were ridiculed as a more confident populace got used to freer sexual activity. But in today's climate of risk-awareness, medical panics about personal safety have returned with a vengeance. Like the grotesque stories about masturbation peddled by doctors in the early century, AIDS-awareness gives a secular, medical form to conservative moralising.

AIDS-awareness is the model of modern-day risk morality. But the dominant theme of AIDS-awareness, the avoidance of risk, extends far beyond the regulation of sexual behaviour. Elevated into the supposedly scientific 'precautionary principle', the conservative message of risk-avoidance is now everywhere reworked in a heady mixture of austerity and humility.

THE PRECAUTIONARY PRINCIPLE

The idea that we should always 'err on the side of caution', has been codified as the 'precautionary principle' and enshrined as a key principle in a number of international agreements, including the UN's Rio Declaration on environment and development of 1992. The Real World Coalition's 'major statement of public concern from over 30 of the UK's leading voluntary and campaigning organisations' puts the case for the precautionary principle to act as a brake on scientific and technological advances where the outcome is 'uncertain':

> That we might cause problems that we cannot solve reinforces the importance of applying the "precautionary principle": erring on the side of environmental safety when risks are large and knowledge uncertain. In some cases this means raising safety standards, in others, simply delaying permission for new technological processes until the consequences are better understood. (*The Politics of the Real World*, 1996, p23)

It is common sense to take steps to prevent obvious problems based on the best available scientific evidence, where this can be done. But, as the above quote indicates, the precautionary principle goes much further than such simple preventative measures. It argues for a halt to new projects or technologies if there is a suspicion that problems might arise. In the introduction to their book *Interpreting the Precautionary Principle,* Timothy O'Riordan and James Cameron add even more restrictions: preventive anticipation—a willingness to take action in advance of scientific proof of a problem; safeguarding ecological space; an assumption that change will be for the worst if risks cannot be quantified; and a duty of care or onus of proof on those who propose change (1994, pp17-18).

Simply stated, the aim is 'the avoidance of unnecessary risk by playing safe' (*Interpreting the Precautionary Principle,* p22).

This idea, that we gain by playing it safe, is central to discussions of science and environmentalism today. Indeed, the call for caution is coming to dominate political and social life as well. Whether the subject be new technologies or sex, caution is presented as a prudent measure in an uncertain world. But is it? There is a major downside: caution means sacrifice and the imposition of limits on what we should attempt to achieve.

The assumption that change will be for the worst is an argument for doing nothing unless we are certain of the outcome in advance. That is a recipe for paralysis. The damaging consequences of applying the precautionary principle in this way are often clearest in the sphere of science and technology, where uncertainty always plays an important part in the acquiring of knowledge. No scientist can know in advance exactly what the outcome of an experiment will be; that is precisely what makes it 'experimental'. The strict application of the precautionary principle in science today would not only lead to sacrifice, it would also deny us the possibility of learning through experimentation.

For an example of the likely conservative effect of insisting upon caution in science, consider the current anxious discussions about genetically modified organisms (GMOs). The release into the wild of genetically modified organisms arouses strong concern today. Environmental writer and campaigner George Monbiot stresses that there is no return once we let them go. In an article entitled 'Mad scientists disease', he warned: 'when a "transgenic" organism has been released into the environment, there may be no means of recalling it if it starts to run amok.' (*Guardian*, 12 December 1995) Dr Sue Mayer, Director of

Science at Greenpeace UK, shares Monbiot's concerns. Invoking the precautionary principle, she argues that GMOs should not be released: 'Although there is no categorical proof that the release of a GMO will be damaging, there is no proof that it is safe. For once, we are trying to prevent damage being done.' (P Wheale and R McNally (eds), *Animal Genetic Engineering: Of Pigs, Oncomice and Men,* 1995, p130)

It all sounds like scary stuff. However, it is a fact that we have many years of experience with GMO release—over 1000 releases in 10 years—without any problems becoming evident that we were unable to deal with. What is more, there have been clear benefits. For example, new crops have been developed which are resistant to herbicides. This allows better control of weeds and increased food output. Virus resistant plants are also being developed. Environmental campaigners want a moratorium on further releases. This would mean missing out on very tangible benefits. It would also deny scientists the opportunity of advancing their knowledge through experiments.

What the precautionary principle is really saying is that we should be so fearful of the unknown and the possible side-effects of our actions that we should risk missing out on the gains that come from new procedures and experimentation. When Ulrich Beck, the German sociologist identified with the concept of the 'risk society', condemns what he calls 'live experiments', and demands the impossible—that scientists must demonstrate safety before they attempt new procedures—he expresses this conservative safety-first outlook in a most striking way (see U Beck, *Ecological Politics in an Age of Risk,* 1995, p123 and p178).

The call for sacrifice which inevitably accompanies the call for caution has some wider implications. The loss of many jobs in the farming industry and the slaughter of thousands of cows, just in case it might possibly turn out that BSE could play a part in causing CJD, is one example. Safety first in life—be it in fewer genetic experiments for fear of Frankenstein or fewer sexual partners for fear of disease—can only breed timidity, encourage conformity, and hold back the human potential for breaking the mould and improving the way things are.

THE USE AND ABUSE OF FUTURE GENERATIONS

One of the major targets of those advocating the precautionary principle is to restrain economic growth and development, in order, they say, to protect the environment. Typically, in their criticism of the European Union for encouraging economic growth, O'Riordan and Cameron issue an explicit call for 'sacrifice' in pursuit of the precautionary principle: 'An unknown number of our actions have incipient global and generational implications. Precaution captures this mood of a new self-interest in collective "sacrifice", namely that good citizenship is both a life-saver and a recognition of solidarity with creation.' (*Interpreting the Precautionary Principle*, p14)

The language employed here is explicitly moralistic, invoking the claims of 'good citizenship' and 'solidarity'. 'Responsibility' is commonly called for, and the argument is given moral weight by highlighting the need to preserve the environment for our children and all the future generations. But, however it is wrapped up, the call for austerity—'sacrifice'—is unmistakable. To gather popular support for sacrifice in the absence of hard data is, they admit, 'one of the most awkward aspects of applying the precautionary principle in a democracy' (p15). But we are left with little doubt that the masses must be forced to come to terms with the sacrifices proposed.

REASONS TO BE SCEPTICAL

The precautionary principle calls for sacrifices. But are these necessary? Are there dangers best avoided and risks best not taken, even if this means passing up on benefits and opportunities? In the case of environmental and scientific issues, there are many reasons to be sceptical of the fears raised by proponents of the principle. In the first instance, many of the problems and risks outlined are greatly exaggerated and some-times entirely invented. And inasmuch as some of the risks might be real, the record shows that humanity is usually well able to deal with problems as they arise. The precautionary principle, it turns out, is premised upon an unwarranted pessimistic assessment of our capacity to deal with all kinds of difficulties. The call for caution and sacrifice sees only problems everywhere, and ignores our potential to come up with solutions.

The call for caution and sacrifice enshrined in the precautionary principle draws heavily upon the environmentalist notion that we are going too far, that humanity is placing too many burdens and stresses upon the environment for sustainable living to continue. Something will give, they say. The growth in car-use has become a focus for these concerns. It is necessary, we are told, to cut back on the car or risk the build up of concentrations of noxious fumes in the atmosphere. Yet the critics of the car appear blind to the quite real possibility of a technical solution which does not depend upon reining in car-use in order to control the emission of poisonous chemicals. Good public transport and less reliance on car-use might be desirable for many reasons, but it is not necessary in order to reduce levels of poisonous substances in the air. Let us look at this discussion a little more closely.

The much-praised *Royal Commission Report on Transport and the Environment* (1994) conjured up the image of a nation covered in roads, suffocated by exhaust fumes. Its central recommendation was the need to reduce reliance on road transport. The report concludes with a quote from the eighteenth-century conservative Edmund Burke's *Reflections on the Revolution in France.* Burke wrote, the report says, that society is 'a partnership not only between those who are living, but between those who are living, those who are dead, and those who are to be born'. For the authors of the report, this captures well the message they want to get across. Current policies, they claim, break this partnership because they breach natural limits—the limits set by finite fuel resources, and the ability of the atmosphere to absorb and disperse pollutants. The car and other aspects of human industry apparently need to be restrained because 'the present genera- tion's cavalier and constantly increasing use of non-renewable resources like oil may well foreclose the options for future generations'. And 'this present transport system is not sustainable because it imposes environmental costs which are so great as to compromise the choices, and the freedom, of future generations'.

However, the science shows that things are not nearly so bad as the report's conclusions would have us believe. The report itself provides plenty of evidence to undermine its own conclusions. It shows that if car-use continued to grow at its present rate, by the year 2020 we would not be suffocating in a cloud of pollutants. On the contrary, catalytic converters, now fitted to all new cars, and the improvements to this technology already in the pipeline, will ensure that atmospheric levels of carbon monoxide, volatile organic compounds, nitrogen oxides, sulphur dioxide, and particulates will all fall by a significant, in some cases drastic, amount, despite there being more cars on the road, all on average travelling further. And this is without considering the possibility of further improvements in technology in the intervening period.

Wrapped up in dubious scientific claims, what is being proposed by the anti-car lobby and other supporters of the precautionary principle is in fact a green, politically correct, austerity package. They want to see measures which would inevitably lead to a reduction in economic growth and reduced living standards for the majority of people in society. This call for sacrifice is excused with a lot of high-minded talk about 'future generations'. But what is really at stake in this discussion is the kind of society we want to see in the present. The invocation of generations to come is not an expression of hope for the future, so much as an injunction to lower our aspirations today. What the supporters of restraint and the precautionary principle refuse to accept is that, above all, people need growth and development now—and that, given free rein, human ingenuity has enormous potential to provide that development. Our first concern ought to be not for the dead or the unborn, but the living and their needs. As far as future generations go, the best legacy we could leave them would surely be a world where human inventiveness and enterprise is allowed to create the wealth and technology to improve the human condition—not one based on the principle of caution, sacrifice and the fear of experimenting or taking risks.

WHAT THE CALL FOR CAUTION REALLY REPRESENTS

The precautionary principle is a means by which to oppose experimentation and call for restraint and self-limitation—a wholly moralistic agenda, in fact. Uncertainty is always played in one direction—that of fearing the worst—and the fantastic spectre of an environmental crisis is a constant presence biasing what might appear to be neutral risk-assessments towards the precautionary end of the spectrum.

Julie Hill's supportive observations on the motives of those who use the precautionary principle to oppose GMO-release demonstrate what lies behind such concerns: 'fear of the possibly catastrophic unknown, together with an instinctive dislike of tampering with nature, helps to reinforce a precautionary approach.' (*Interpreting the Precautionary Principle,* p175) Notice anything missing here? Hill's case makes no mention of the known facts about GMO-release or the years of scientific experience of such releases on which an assessment could be based. Instead her argument is based entirely on a predisposition to mistrust change, an assumption that any human intervention in nature can only be for the worse. Hill revels in uncertainty, citing a general fear of the unknown and an instinctive dislike of tampering with nature. In another time, such sentiments which divorce belief from a rational assessment of reality would be called superstition. Today, however, the religion of the precautionary principle can intervene in serious scientific issues to legitimise the agenda of restraint.

The fact that scientific opinion and experimentation always contains an element of uncertainty is being latched on to as a way of arguing against deliberate action for a particular end, and assuming that the worst will happen. For example, in 1995, when Shell tried to dump the Brent Spar oil platform in the North Sea, the environmental group Greenpeace launched an international campaign to stop it. Greenpeace did not have the evidence or the arguments to support its emotional opposition to Shell's plans, so it played what the journal *Nature* described as 'the trump card of uncertainty' (7 March 1996), arguing that dumping the Brent Spar at sea could cause unforeseen damage. Greenpeace's claims were later exposed as unfounded, and the organisation had to apologise for getting its facts wrong. But, no matter that it had been an irrational exercise built on prejudice, the important thing for Greenpeace was that the campaign to stop the Brent Spar being dumped at sea had succeeded. Greenpeace's use of uncertainty to demand caution is mirrored by many others today.

Ulrich Beck has built a whole sociological outlook based on this irrational procedure. Linking BSE to Chernobyl and the dangers posed by genetic engineering, Beck has warned that 'we are in danger of creating a situation where alarmingly large risks are nobody's responsibility'. 'Neglecting risks', he suggests, 'is one of the most effective ways of reinforcing them' ('When experiments go wrong', *Independent,* 26 March 1996).

Beck's analysis, like that of Greenpeace over the Brent Spar, uses uncertainty to build in an inflation of risks. He then calls on this pre-inflated sense of risk to cast doubt on the usefulness of social and scientific progress, as well as the ability of humanity to cope with change. Beck makes it clear that his theory of a 'risk society' is premised upon the possibility of the ultimate worst-case scenario—human extinction: 'I use the term "risk society"', he writes, 'for those societies that are confronted by the challenges of the self-created possibility, hidden at first, then increasingly apparent, of the self-destruction of all life on this earth' (*Ecological Politics in an Age of Risk,* p67). But just what might bring this about? Well, almost anything in the fantasy land of Beck. The abstract postulation of the possibility of extinction gives him the licence to go about discussing new procedures in a fearful tone and inflating and conflating all known risks—from BSE to the fall-out from Chernobyl.

The facts of the matter do not much concern Beck. By playing on uncertainty, he absolves himself of any obligation to respond to those who outline hard evidence refuting him. This methodology belittles the importance of human knowledge in the face of super-stitious fears of the unknown. Risks are said to be uncertain on account of unforeseen consequences. Yet we are told to restrain the experimental urges of scientists until they can quantify these unquantifiable risks. This can only mean that novel technologies and procedures should not be tried since 'uncertain' risks can never entirely be foreseen. The consequences of the increasingly influential line of argument developed by Beck and his fellow thinkers is that we are robbed of any chance of learning from our actions. Caution is elevated into the prime directive of all action, and the possibility of solving problems by developing new techniques is dismissed in advance. Risk-avoidance may come in the trappings of expert advice, but it is profoundly hostile to rational investigation and inquiry. But then, the precautionary principle is not science at all, but a religious and moral code for our time.

BRINGING GOD BACK IN

The various attempts by the politicians to reimpose a moral code are bound to fail. Moralism is not something that can be summoned up out of a hat. Revitalising the church, whether through hellfire preaching or New Age services is unlikely to succeed either. Collective worship and a traditional God have little appeal in today's secular and often cynical age. Nor was it likely that the positive promotion of the free market as a moral order could be successful. Without economic success to underpin it, free market individualism raises more problems than it resolves. But that does not mean that contemporary capitalism is bereft of any moral code whatsoever. Only that the moral restraints of today must of necessity match the times.

Today's emerging moral order rests on quite distinct premises. It is the climate of fear and anxiety that underpins contemporary moral restraints. Risk-avoidance and the precautionary principle are at the core of latter-day moralising. In the past we were told to fear divine retribution. Today, the coercion is no less other-worldly, but is presented in secular terms. Personal safety and the safety of the planet stand in the place of the divine.

Like the religious values that preceded it, the precautionary principle is an expression of man's loss of control of his own destiny. As human agency is lost in the climate of fear, precaution weighs in as a heavy constraint on man's hubris. Like the religious values that preceded it, the precautionary principle rests on an ineffable being. Not God this time but a ubiquitous risk resists all rational investigation and paralyses human action. Fear of an all-embracing and limitless risk is quite as debilitating as religious obscurantism ever could be.

Like the religious values that preceded it, the precautionary principle acts as a moral constraint in the service of the status quo. Fear of change is pervasive when precaution is the guiding principle. Conservatism and moderation are the outcome of the precautionary principle in a way that serves to sanctify the status quo against all possible change and development. And finally, like the religious values that preceded it, the precautionary principle serves as an apology for an inhuman society. All of the barriers to change and improvement that were once expressed in religious terms are today eloquently reformulated in the secular terminology of risk-avoidance. Where all attempts to develop society and better man's lot in the world are presented as inherently dangerous to personal safety and to the safety of the planet, the pressure is on to do as little as possible to upset the delicate balance of the ecological order.

The struggle to liberate men and women today must begin with a struggle to liberate them from the modern obscurantism of risk and the precautionary principle. On that score we can at least be thankful that reason and a muscular common sense can readily dispel the perverse fears of a pervasive and unknowable 'risk'—if only we are confident enough to make them our standard.

THE DANGERS OF CAUTION

The contemporary discussion about morality raises caution to a guiding principle of life. The pervasive consciousness of risk, the assumption that the worst is always likely to happen, informs how the public and the professional commentators react to events today. It is in effect a powerful moral code without ever being announced as such. Like all moral codes, the morals of caution reveal most about how people are supposed to think about themselves.

The celebration of safety, alongside the continuous warning about risks, constitutes a profoundly anti-human intellectual and ideological regime. It continually invites society and its individual members to constrain their aspirations and to limit their actions. The call for restraint and lowering our sights can now be heard everywhere, be it in discussions of science, school results or living standards. The continuous lowering of expectations can be justified through an exaggerated presentation of the destructive side of science and technology, or through the projection of people as fragile individuals, who cannot be expected to cope with anything too drastic or different.

The advocacy of safety and the rejection of risk-taking

has important implications for us all. If experimentation is discredited, society effectively acknowledges its inability to tackle—never mind to solve—the problems which confront it. The restrictions being placed on experimentation, in the name of protecting us and our children from risk, actually represent the dissipation of the human potential.

The paradox is that the search for safety is bound to backfire. Throughout history, greater safety and security have always been the by-products of innovation and experimentation. Life has become safer as human society has progressed and mastered nature. Safety was not something that could be acquired just by wanting it. Those who propose to avoid risks and gain safety will invariably find that what they acquire instead are obsessions. On the contrary, it is the extension of human control through social and scientific experimentation and change that has provided societies with greater security than before.

Today the fear of taking risks is creating a society that celebrates victimhood rather than heroism. We are all expected to compete, like guests on *Oprah,* to prove that we are the most put-upon and pathetic people in the house, the most deserving of counselling and compensation. The virtues held up to be followed are passivity rather than activism, safety rather than boldness. And the rather diminished individual that emerges is indulged on the grounds that, in a world awash with new medical conditions and crises and impending catastrophe, he or she is doing a good job just by surviving.

Perhaps the most powerful expression of this mood of caution is the widespread denunciation of ambition and drive as selfishness. It is a commonplace today to look back upon the 1980s as a decade of greed that went too far. The economic policies pursued by Margaret Thatcher in Britain or Ronald Reagan in America are seen to have elevated material success over communal ties, and to have left the weak to suffer while the strong thrived. It is argued that the slump at the beginning of the 1990s was a necessary consequence of the greed-fuelled boom of the late eighties; excessive buying on credit was one long party that was bound to end in a hangover because we were all living beyond our means (see D Smith, *From Boom to Bust: Trial and Error in British Economic Policy,* 1992, or K Phillips, *The Politics of Rich and Poor,* 1991). The popular version of this argument is exemplified by Oliver Stone's caricature of the acquisitive trader Gordon Gekko in the film *Wall Street,* who proclaims to an audience of shareholders that 'Greed is good'. For the audience in the cinema this is a *reductio ad absurdum* of free market morality.

The philosophy of the 'caring nineties', with its emphasis upon individuals showing caution, concern and restraint for the good of the community, has been presented as an antidote to the 'greedy eighties'. The appeal of this version of events is that it translates social and economic issues into a moral parable. However, a great deal is lost in the translation. The moral tale distorts what really went on in the eighties, and sends out a perverse message for today in the process.

The events of the 1980s bear only a passing resemblance to the parable. Most working people succeeded in maintaining or improving their living standards, not by taking it easy on the never-never, but by working harder and longer. The number of two-income households increased in the eighties, as did working hours. The slump of the nineties may have followed on inevitably from the short-lived boom of the eighties. But that was down to the money men in the City of London and other big capitalists, who built a house of cards by speculating billions of pounds on paper assets to make a quick profit. It had nothing to do with the 'greediness' of the mass of ordinary people.

The parable of the 'greedy eighties' and the 'caring nineties' is not just historically inaccurate. It is the vehicle for an objectionable moral code for the present. People who spent the eighties trying to improve the living standards of themselves and their families, for example by making enough money to pay the mortgage on a semi-detached house rather than rent a council flat, are now branded as greedy and selfish. It is as if having a credit card now makes you a capitalist exploiter. The underlying message is that we must all rein in our acquisitiveness and settle for less; not because a stagnant economic system has less to offer us today, you understand, but because it is the morally correct thing to do.

A particularly grotesque proposition contained in today's moral parable is that the greedy majority are somehow responsible for the sufferings of the poor. According to the prestigious Rowntree Trust, for example, the problems of poverty are exacerbated by the division between work-rich and work-poor families. It notes that many families have two incomes while a minority have none. By implication, the greedy majority have taken all the work away from the poverty-stricken few, and they should surely make some sacrifices to help those less well off.

But just let us look at that proposition again. 'Work-rich'?

The very term suggests that hard work is some kind of privilege, and jobs are riches that are monopolised by the majority at the expense of the minority. As if the fact that both partners go to work to maintain their living standards should be seen as a shameful indulgence, an extravagant luxury. Working hard because you want a better life is not the same as 'riches', and nor should it be seen as a bad thing. The consequence of this perverse moralism is to turn a problem created by the capitalist market—the abject poverty which afflicts a minority—into a moral failing of ordinary people, and to demand sacrifices from us all.

Out of this twisted telling of the tale comes an equally perverse set of values and moral judgements. Without doubt the unalloyed celebration of the market in the 1980s left something to be desired. In many ways, though, the moral critique of the greedy eighties gives rise to an even worse outlook, based on a low estimation of the human potential for improvement.

The idea that you should want to better your condition is caricatured as 'greed'. The idea that you should aspire to greater personal freedom is decried as selfishness and an insensibility to the sufferings of your fellow man. In this view, the most basic motive of man throughout the ages, the aspiration to improve the conditions of life, which has driven humanity from the caves to civilisation, is vilified.

On the face of it this might sound like a criticism of capitalism. In fact it relocates the failings of a particular system of social organisation on to humanity in general. Of course there are better ways to realise human ambition than subordinating every activity to the chaotic judgements of the market and the demands of the laws of profit. But that is not the new moralists' point. Rather, what is being argued is that ambition itself is at fault. Man's hubris, in science and technology, in the arts and economics, is the problem. Which is why modesty, caution, restraint and sacrifice are lauded as the virtues of the caring nineties.

Some virtue. You do not have to be an apologist for capitalism to understand that ambition and the aspiration for a better life are powerful forces for social advancement, which should be tapped rather than condemned. Indeed the great failing of the market system in the past 25 years has been its inability to give human ingenuity and enterprise its due. The most creative endeavours of the modern age have tended to project beyond the narrow interests of making profits, from the cultural upheavals of the early century to the conquest of space or the development of the Internet today. Where people have reached for the stars, capital investment and capitalist courage have been wanting.

In these conditions we have two choices. We could turn our backs on ingenuity and ambition, and get used to living within the limitations imposed by the cautious moral code of our time— a code which just happens to coincide with the generally undynamic state of capitalism today. Or we could do the opposite. Instead of reining in our ambitions to suit the social conditions of the day, we could set about trying to transform those conditions. If creativity and emancipation are off the agenda, isn't it time to rewrite the agenda? If society dictates that we cannot have what we want for a decent life, isn't it time to change society?

A world that was peopled by the kind of shrinking violets envisaged in the morals of caution would be a sorry place.

It would be a world where success meant winning the sympathy of your fellow men, where suffering and victimhood were badges of honour, and assertiveness was despised. But what if we embrace a different set of values, where self-confidence, self-respect and autonomy are seen as positive qualities, and people earn their authority by virtue of their actions? Where the accepted dogma today is caution and safety, men and women would be better served if they embraced the challenges and even the risks of overturning that dogma and shaking up the stagnant society that gave rise to it.

The culture of limits and the morality of caution are not just interesting ideas to be thought about. They are major problems to be fought against—and they are made all the more dangerous by the fact that they are so rarely recognised as problems at all. The aim of this book has been to bring to public attention these major problems of our time. Those of us who still believe that we can improve the human condition, and that tomorrow does not have to be like today, now have a duty to do something about cracking them. Spreading the message of the *Manifesto for a World Fit for People* is as good a place to start as any.

A MANIFESTO FOR A WORLD FIT FOR PEOPLE

We live in a world where excuses masquerade as knowledge and wisdom. It has become fashionable to inflate the slightest difficulty into a problem of cosmological dimensions. Routine problems are represented as portents of extinction. This obsession with risks and perils has served to justify restraint, austerity and low expectations. Terms like 'sustainable' and 'self-limiting' have come to symbolise a society which has accepted survival as an end in itself.

※ ※ ※ ※

It is ironic that capitalism, which has traditionally been associated with materialism and the promise of unlimited wealth creation, now finds refuge in the humble rhetoric of sustainable development. The lowering of expectations not just in the economy, but in every area of life reflects how insecure capitalists now feel about their own mission.

※ ※ ※ ※

Unfortunately, in the absence of any alternative, the lack of capitalist self-belief has been generalised as a failure of nerve throughout society as whole. At every level of society there is fear of change. Such fears are expressed through the contemporary obsession with personal health and safety and with preserving the environment. These concerns often appear as a critique of greed and excess—hence the popularity of dumping on the 'greedy eighties'. However such criticism of greed all too often turns out to be an attack on any human ambition for improvement.

※ ※ ※ ※

As Marxists we could go on about poverty, exploitation, and the lack of opportunities open to most people. We could talk about the system of imperialist domination which continues to run the world. There is little doubt that a system narrowly based on profit-creation conflicts with the interests of humanity as a whole. However, there is little point in rehearsing these arguments today. We face some new and far-reaching problems, the most important of which is humanity's lack of belief in itself—in its potential to solve the problems of society and in its unbounded power of creativity.

❖ ❖ ❖ ❖

To create a world fit for people we need to mobilise all those who are not prepared to accept today's culture of limits. To that end we need to wage a struggle of ideas against the conservative intellectual climate which influences the entire political spectrum. A hundred years ago, it was the forces of religion which sought to hold back humanity's progress. Today, the old religion has been discredited. Instead we have new philosophies that denounce 'man's arrogance'. Others question the role of science and knowledge and accuse humanity of going too far. Fashionable gurus advise that we should consume less and restrain our passions.

❖ ❖ ❖ ❖

Our reply to all of the pleas for caution and restraint is that until now humanity has only learned to crawl. We still live in a world that is not fit for people. Our problem is not that we are too ambitious, but that we continually hesitate about experimenting with new solutions. We need a revolution in outlook, so that we can continue to advance and give new scope to human creativity.

❖ ❖ ❖ ❖

What we face is not just a battle of ideas. Those who counsel restraint and moderation do not merely rely on words. The entire political system has been converted into an authoritarian mould where dissent is punished as surely as the heresies of the past. The state intervenes in areas of life hitherto left untouched.

❖ ❖ ❖ ❖

Alongside the battle of ideas, we will need to fight against all of the new rules and codes which are designed to regulate and constrain individual action. The enforcement of the culture of limits by the state demands a response that draws on the political and intellectual resources of all those who remain committed to the project of human progress.

SO WHAT'S YOUR ALTERNATIVE?

If you have any ideas, questions or arguments about the issues dealt with in *The Point Is to Change It,* we want to hear from you.

Living Marxism is keen to see as wide a debate as possible around the new agenda we need to set now. The discussion about the future of the society in which we all live is much too important to be left to the politicians and the pundits.

Better still, if you like what you have read so far, you can help us to develop the ideas outlined in the book, and spread the message of the manifesto.

**Write to: Manifesto, *Living Marxism*,
BM RCP, London WC1N 3XX.
Or you can e-mail us at lm@junius.co.uk**

The discussion will be continuing in the pages of *Living Marxism* and on our Web site (see over for details).

Living Marxism
ONLINE

Netscape: Living Marxism Online

Back | Forward | Home | Reload | Images | Open | Print | Find | Stop

Go To: http://www.junius.co.uk/home.html

What's New? | What's Cool? | Handbook | Net Search | Net Directory | Newsgroups

LIVING

Living Marxism Online. Developing a radical agenda for change in an age of lowered expectations. Living Marxism stands for progress against green technophobia, and for emancipation in a climate of increasing social regulation. Our aim is a human-centred politics that makes no concessions to the victim culture or the fear of a risk-obsessed society. We expose the hidden truth behind Western intervention in the third world. Join the debate.

DISCUSS: LM commentaries | Discussions | Chat | Events

RESEARCH: LM search | LM index | External links

TRANSACT: Bookstore | LM subscriptions

HIGHLIGHTS
Current | LM commentary | Conference | Next Chat: 15 May 20.30 BST
magazine | War crimes trials | The WEEK | What's wrong with masculinity?

Problems & Suggestions

All material © RCP

http://www.junius.co.uk